How to Win at Financial Spread Betting

FT Prentice Hall
FINANCIAL TIMES

In an increasingly competitive world, we believe it's quality of thinking that will give you the edge – an idea that opens new doors, a technique that solves a problem, or an insight that simply makes sense of it all. The more you know, the smarter and faster you can go.

That's why we work with the best minds in business and finance to bring cutting-edge thinking and best learning practice to a global market.

Under a range of leading imprints, including *Financial Times Prentice Hall*, we create world-class print publications and electronic products bringing our readers knowledge, skills and understanding which can be applied whether studying or at work.

To find out more about our business publications, or tell us about the books you'd like to find, you can visit us at
www.business-minds.com

For other Pearson Education publications, visit
www.pearsoned-ema.com

INVESTOR'S GUIDE

How to Win at Financial Spread Betting

CHARLES VINTCENT

FINANCIAL TIMES

An imprint of **Pearson Education**

London · New York · San Francisco · Toronto · Sydney · Tokyo · Singapore
Hong Kong · Cape Town · Madrid · Paris · Milan · Munich · Amsterdam

PEARSON EDUCATION LIMITED

Head Office:
Edinburgh Gate
Harlow CM20 2JE
Tel: +44 (0)1279 623623
Fax: +44 (0)1279 431059

London Office:
128 Long Acre
London WC2E 9AN
Tel: +44 (0)20 7447 2000
Fax: +44 (0)20 7447 2170
Website: www.financialminds.com

....

First published in Great Britain in 2002

© Pearson Education Limited 2002

The right of Charles Vintcent to be identified as Author
of this Work has been asserted by him in accordance
with the Copyright, Designs and Patents Act 1988.

ISBN 0 273 65413 6

British Library Cataloguing in Publication Data
A CIP catalogue record for this book can be obtained from the British Library.

10 9 8 7 6 5 4

Typeset by Northern Phototypesetting Co Ltd, Bolton
Printed and bound in Great Britain by Biddles Ltd, Guildford & King's Lynn

The Publishers' policy is to use paper manufactured from sustainable forests.

About the author

Charles Vintcent has been a practising private client stockbroker since 1982. He has worked in the City since 1964, gaining investment experience with the Charterhouse Group, Hambros Bank and Cannon Assurance Ltd. He is chairman of International SC, trading as International Spread Betting. Charles was born in India, educated at Charterhouse and commissioned into the 16th/5th Queens Royal Lancers.

Contents

PART TWO Winning techniques using financial spread betting

Acknowledgements

I am indebted to David Linton and the team at Updata Software Ltd for their help and programs which enabled me to reproduce the graphics, and for their clear and lucid training sessions. Also, for the help and 'editing' of the technical details received from Charles Knot and David Buik of Cantor Index for unravelling the complexities of betting from the point of view of the bookmaker. Lastly for the help and support of Wendy.

Introduction

Financial spread betting is the fastest growing sector in the investment field today. It is significant that within the last year, the number of financial bookmakers has increased from two to six, and there are more to come.

There are a number of substantial benefits to be enjoyed by using financial spread betting, and this book will tell you all about them. You will be better informed by understanding what financial spread betting is, and how it works. Knowledge is valuable, and you will be able to harness your knowledge to help you make money.

Many people are frightened away from financial spread betting because they are convinced that the whole thing is very risky, and that they might lose a great deal of money. Experience has proved that this view tends to be held by those who do not fully understand what spread betting is all about, and who have never learned how to make the investment work for them. There is risk attached, but no more so than investing in futures, options or any other instrument in the derivatives market, and it is perfectly possible to control the exposure to risk and limit your liability to loss, which is more than can be said for investing in shares. This book will teach you the techniques of protecting your wealth, as well as showing you how to increase your profits.

Under current legislation, all winnings obtained from financial spread betting are completely free from both income tax and capital gains tax, and this is a benefit that is well worth having. No responsible financial adviser should ever recommend an investment solely on the grounds that it is tax efficient, but nevertheless the benefit of complete freedom from any tax whatsoever is hard to beat. This advantage is increased considerably when you use financial spread betting as a fail-safe adjunct to your portfolio of ordinary shares to protect your capital against a falling share price. Not only can you use financial spread betting as a hedge against reducing values in your equity port-folio, but also this investment allows you to make money in a falling market by going 'short' of a share, or index, which is impossible under modern share dealing practices. This book will enhance your range of investment techniques and enable you to harness the technical advances that have been achieved by using on-line dealing facilities to take advan-tage of fast moving markets and short term trading opportunities that are impossible otherwise.

If used properly, financial spread betting is no more risky than any other investment in securities, and often it is much more profitable over a shorter period. You cannot afford to miss the opportunities that finan-cial spread betting opens up for you. You should be able to smile all the way to the bank.

What is
financial
spread betting?

Part One explains what financial spread betting involves, how it works and what are the risks. It describes in detail the two different types of bet that you can use. They are intraday bets, and futures based bets. The text takes you through the construction of these bets step-by-step for two reasons.

First, many people find the concept somewhat confusing when they first start to use financial spread betting, and it is a natural reaction to mistrust something that you do not completely understand. There are risks, but if you are aware of both the reasons why you may be exposed to them, as well as knowing how to control your potential liabilities, you should avoid becoming financially embarrassed.

Second, unless you really understand how the whole operation works you will be at a huge disadvantage compared to those who do. It is only by being able to use the tremendous flexibility of financial spread betting, as well as harnessing the gearing that it provides, that you can really benefit financially from this exciting and absorbing investment method.

In Part One you will learn that you have a choice between two types of bet that appear to be similar, but which carry their own different pros and cons.

- Intraday bets die at the end of a day's trading period and you either win or lose over a very short time.

- Futures based bets give you more time to leave the bet open and for the price to recover if initially it moves against you. However, you may have to put up extra margin payments for this type of bet whilst it remains open.

The ability to close either type of bet at any time remains with you so that you can limit your potential loss.

Part Two describes various winning techniques for you to use, after you have mastered the mechanics of financial spread betting.

1

Financial spread betting and conventional betting: a comparison

Conventional betting
Financial spread betting
The different types of financial spread betting
Dealing costs – financial spread betting v buying shares

In this chapter we explain:

- the difference between financial spread betting and conventional betting
- dealing costs – financial spread betting v buying shares.

CONVENTIONAL BETTING

Most of us know how betting on horses or dogs works. Financial spread betting is different.

When you place a win bet on a horse, or a dog, at a race meeting, you decide which of the entrants for the race will run faster than the others over a specific distance, and the animal you have chosen will be the first past the post, or be among the first two or three, if you have backed it for a place. After you have studied the form and perhaps considered the merits of the different selections of the tipsters, you make your choice and then check the odds being offered by the bookmakers to find one that is making the best price against your particular nomination for that race. You make the choice, and the bookmaker offers odds against your selection being the first to pass the post, or achieve a place. When you place a bet, you are entering into a contract which runs from the moment the bet is agreed until the race is over. You cannot reduce your liability part way through the race. Nor can you claim a profit whilst the race is in progress, should your horse or dog be temporarily leading the field, and you cannot cancel any further interest in the remainder of the race or its final outcome. You cannot close the bet at any time after it has been laid. The bet runs until the race is ended.

If your bet was for a 'win' only, you will lose all your stake if your selection does not come first past the post. Similarly, if your bet was for a 'place', you will lose unless your selection was in the first two or three to finish.

FINANCIAL SPREAD BETTING

Financial spread betting differs fundamentally from conventional betting in that there is no 'finishing post' in the normal sense, although there is a time limit involved. It is not a question of one company's share, or an index such as the FTSE 100 for example, beating all comers within a specific period of time. Quite simply, *you* decide whether you think that a particular share price, or the level of an index, will be higher or lower up to a fixed date in the future than the price that the bookmaker is quoting, and you place your bet accordingly.

A bookmaker will predict where a financial market will stand at a specified time in the future. That prediction takes the form of a spread – the range between the high and the low prices that he might be quoting.

If you think that the share price, or the index, is going to go up, you back your judgement by placing a 'buy' bet with a bookmaker. If you think it will go down, you place a 'sell' bet.

There are two huge advantages to financial spread betting, among several others. One is that you can close down your bet at any time you like, and as soon as you like, after having made the contract with the bookmaker. You could close it down five minutes later, if you wish, so *you* are in control of your exposure to risk. The second is that you can make profits in a falling market. Since it is pretty well impossible to 'short' a share on the London market nowadays, unless you employ financial spread betting for your benefit you will not be able to capitalize on the opportunity of making money out of a falling share price.

> **you can close down your bet at any time you like**

THE DIFFERENT TYPES OF FINANCIAL SPREAD BETTING

There are two different types of financial spread betting, and they are fundamentally similar, except that the period over which the bet can run is substantially different. They may be described briefly as follows.

- *'Intraday' bets.* An intraday bet can be contracted at any time during market hours, but unless instructions are given to close it before the market shuts, it will close automatically at that time. These bets are based on your opinion of the probable movement of an individual share price, or an index, upwards or downwards during the market hours remaining for that day.

- *'Futures' based bets.* These bets are based on your opinion of whether the price of an individual share, or the level of an index, will be above or below the figure quoted by the financial bookmaker on the next quarter day, or the one after that. You choose whether you want to let the bet run until the quarter day selected, or whether you want to close it before that date.

We shall examine these different types of spread bets in detail later on in the book.

DEALING COSTS – FINANCIAL SPREAD BETTING V BUYING SHARES

When you buy or sell a share through the London Stock Exchange, there are various costs and charges that are payable, as well as various forms or records that have to be completed. Most of these do not apply when you make a financial spread bet. Figure 1.1 compares the requirements for the two investments.

Name of form/charge	Share	Financial spread bet
Contract note	Yes	Yes
Government stamp duty		
On purchase	Yes	No
On sale	No	No
Share certificate or electronic register	Yes	No
Charge for nominee A/c register	In some cases	No
Administration charge	In some cases	No
Signed transfer form for delivery on sale	Yes	No

FIG 1.1   **Comparing the requirements for two investments**

Contract note

This record is an essential document in any financial transaction, since it describes in detail what was executed by the stockbroker or financial bookmaker on behalf of the client, and it forms the basis for any subsequent dispute. You should always get a contract note sent to you at the end of each day, whether you buy or sell a share, or open or close a financial spread bet. The contract note should show the following details for each transaction:

In the case of a share:

- the full name of the security and its denomination, e.g. 25p ordinary
- the statement 'bought' or 'sold'
- the number of shares bought or sold
- the price at which the bargain was struck
- the costs and any charges itemized
- the total cost or net amount receivable from the transaction

- the time that the bargain was executed.

In the case of a financial spread bet:

- the currency in which the bet is traded, e.g. GBP
- the share or index on which the bet is laid
- the futures date when the bet expires (unless it is closed out before)
- the date and time that the bet was placed
- the description of the opening bet, e.g. buy or sell
- the amount of the stake
- the bet/trade reference number
- the same details as above for the closing bet together with the reference number of the opening trade/bet
- the closing balance.

In the case of partial closing, the remaining open position(s) will be described. Similarly, if the original opening bet is closed out by several different closing bets at different times, or on different days, all the relevant details shown above will be itemized on the account.

As far as the rest of the costs, charges and forms required are concerned, there is no comparison between the two types of transaction. There are significant differences between the two, and substantial benefits for you, the investor:

- no charges levied by the government in the form of stamp duty for financial spread betting;
- no certificates are issued;
- no register for details of ownership;
- no transfer forms to be delivered before winnings are paid;
- no administration charges levied by the financial bookmaker;
- no charges for nominee accounts, depots or safekeeping.

Summary

In this chapter we have examined:

■ The difference between conventional betting and financial spread betting, and shown that, whereas conventional betting is based on 'first past the post', financial spread betting is based on your opinion that the price of a share, or an index, will be higher or lower than the bookmaker is predicting at a date in the future.

■ The different types of financial spread betting, such as intraday or futures based bets, together with the comparisons of costs for each type.

2

Structure of financial spread betting

What is a financial spread bet?
How does it work?
Gearing
What is the 'spread'?
What is the bookmaker's charge?
Who pays the betting tax?

In this chapter we explain the basic structure of financial spread betting. In particular we provide answers to the following questions:

- What is a financial spread bet?
- How does it work?
- What is the 'spread'?
- What is the bookmaker's charge?
- Who pays the betting tax?

WHAT IS A FINANCIAL SPREAD BET?

If you think that the price of a specific share, or the level of an index, such as the FTSE 100 or the Dow Jones Industrial Average, will be higher or lower than it is at this time, you place an 'up bet', or a 'down bet', now. If you place an 'up bet', and the price, or level moves up, you win. If it moves down, you lose.

If you believe that the share price, or the index level will rise, and you want to follow your judgement by betting that it will go up, you use the word 'buy', rather than up bet. Similarly, if you think the price will go down, you use the word 'sell' rather than down bet. Thus you would tell the bookmaker that you want to buy or sell the share or index at the time that you place the bet.

When you contact the bookmaker to get a price, he will quote two different prices to you, e.g. 6324, at 6330. The difference between the two prices is the spread. We explain this in more detail later on in this chapter.

✳ EXAMPLE

You believe that the FTSE 100 index will move up, and so you decide to buy. If you open a bet by 'buying', you close it by 'selling'. You decide to stake £5 per point that the index rises from its current level of 6330. It rises, so you decide to close your bet and take a profit.

Opening 'buy'	£5 @ 6330
Closing 'sell'	£5 @ 6362
Points difference	32
Profit	£5 x 32 = £160

However, if the index had fallen to a level below 6330 when you closed out the bet, you would have *lost* £5 x the points difference between the opening and closing prices of the FTSE 100 index.

If you place a 'buy' bet, the more the price rises, the more you win. If you place a 'buy' bet, the more the price falls, the more you lose. Similarly, if you think that the price is likely to drop, you place a 'sell' bet to open. If it does drop, you win.

You believe that the FTSE 100 index will move down, and so you decide to sell. If you open a bet by 'selling', you close it by 'buying'. You decide to stake £5 per point that the index falls from its current level of 6330. It falls so you decide to close your bet and take a profit.

Opening 'sell'	£5 @ 6330
Closing 'buy'	£5 @ 6295
Points difference	35
Profit	£5 x 35 = £175

However, if the index had risen to a level above 6330 when you closed out the bet, you would have *lost* £5 x the points difference between the opening and closing prices of the FTSE 100 index.

If you place a 'sell' bet, the more the price falls, the more you win. If you place a 'sell' bet, the more the price rises, the more you lose.

HOW DOES IT WORK?

When you place the bet, you will specify the amount of money that you want to stake *per point* that the index level rises, if you are placing a 'buy' bet, or falls if you are placing a 'sell' bet. If you bet on the movement of a share price, you decide on the amount of the stake *per penny* that the share will rise or fall.

Let us assume that you decide to bet that the price of a share in XYZ plc will rise from its current price of 240p. You place a 'buy' bet at £10 per penny at that level. That means that you win £10 for every 1p that the price rises above 240p. The 'point, or unit of measurement' in every case is the denomination in which the instrument is traded, e.g. pence, cents,

F.Fr., D-Marks, Euro denominated shares etc. You specify how much in Pounds (£), US Dollars ($) or Euros (E) you wish to stake as your bet per point movement in the market.

Suppose that the price rises to 256p, and you close the bet at that level.

Bought   XYZ plc @ 240p x £10 per penny
Sold   XYZ plc @ 256p (to close the previous opening bet).

$$256p$$
$$-240p$$

Profit 16p x £10 / p = £160

If the price had gone the other way, you would lose by the same amount of the stake per penny.

However, suppose that the price had fallen to 229p and you closed your bet at that level.

Bought   XYZ plc @ 240p x £10 per penny
Sold   XYZ plc @ 229p x £10 per penny (to close the previous opening bet).

$$240p$$
$$-229p$$

Loss 11p x £10 / p = £110

Exactly the same principles apply if you place a 'sell' bet. Let us assume that the share price of ABC plc is currently 504p, and you think that it is overpriced and will fall. You place a 'sell' bet at that level at £10 per penny.

Suppose that the price falls to 482p and you close your bet at that level.

Sold   ABC plc @ 504p x £10 per penny
Bought   ABC plc @ 482p x £10 per penny (to close the previous opening bet).

$$504p$$
$$-482p$$

Profit 22p x £10 / p = £220

However, suppose the price goes the wrong way from your point of view, and it rises to 524p so you decide to close the bet at that level, rather than incur any further loss.

Sold   ABC plc @ 504p x £10 per penny
Bought   ABC plc @ 524p x £10 per penny (to close the previous open-
            ing bet).

524p

–504p

Loss 20p x £10 / p = £200

An important point should be emphasized at this juncture. You will see from the examples given so far that I have said that 'you decide to close your bet at that level'. It is one of the great advantages of financial spread betting that you remain in control of some of the risk factors while your bet is open. You can decide to close your bet at any time you like and there are no costs or charges or financial penalties for so doing. We shall return to this vital element later on in this book.

> **You can decide
> to close your bet
> at any time**

The examples given above illustrate the essential difference between financial spread betting and any other sort of fixed odds betting, which is that you are able to back your judgement by placing a bet that a share price or index level will rise or fall over a period in the future, and that you can either crystallize your winnings or cancel any further liability to loss at any time that you choose. You do *not* have to wait until 'the end of the race' to find out your financial result.

GEARING

The high level of gearing enables you to trade in much greater quantities than would be the case if you had to pay for the shares in full. Consequently, although this factor allows you to make considerably larger returns on the capital employed, the risk of loss is increased similarly.

✱ EXAMPLE

Freeserve is standing at 123p. For the purpose of this example, let us assume there is no bid/offer spread either for the share price or for the spread bet price.

You could buy 1000 shares for £1230 (excluding commissions, stamp duty and dealing costs).

Capital employed		£
Outright purchase (1000 shares @ 123p)		1230
Financial spread bet (buy @ £10 per penny)		NIL

Share price rises 20p to 143p		*Return on capital employed %*
Profit on outright purchase (1000 x 20p)	200	16.26
Profit on financial spread bet (£10 x 20p)	200	200.0

However, if the share price had gone the other way, although there would have been a paper loss in the value of the holding purchased outright, which would only have become an actual loss if the holding was sold at that point, the investor employing financial spread betting would have had to absorb an actual loss of £200 if the spread bet expired at that price level.

Do not confuse return on capital employed with risk ...

WHAT IS THE 'SPREAD'?

The spread is the difference between the bid and offer price that the bookmaker quotes when you ask for the price of a share or an index.

For example, let us take the mid price of a share in Boots as being 505p. If you ask the bookmaker for a price, you might be quoted '502, at 508'. You will be expected to know that the quotation is in sterling and in pence.

It is very important that you understand the 'shorthand' in the way that the prices are quoted, and exactly what they mean, so that you don't get confused and make potentially expensive mistakes. It is not difficult, and you will soon get to understand the language.

A 'bid' price is one that someone is prepared to pay for something: an 'offer' price is that at which someone is prepared to sell something.

Thus, when the bookmaker is making a price of '502 (his bid), at 508', the lower one is the price that *he* is prepared to accept a *sell bet from you at that moment* for a share in Boots. As far as you are concerned, the *bid* price is always the one at which *you* can *sell* to the bookmaker.

> **you will soon get to understand the language**

He is 'offering the stock' at 508. *He* is prepared to *sell a bet to you at that moment* for a share in Boots at that price. From your point of view, the price at which the share is *offered* is the one that *you* can *buy* from the bookmaker.

It is easy to remember – for example, the quote '6p , at 10p' means you *sell* **to** him for 6p, and you *buy* **from** him at 10p, or £s or US$ or whatever the currency is in which the share, index or commodity is being traded. You will see the importance of this when we discuss how to conduct financial spread betting in Chapter 3.

WHAT IS THE BOOKMAKER'S CHARGE?

The bookmaker levies his charge from within the spread between the bid and offer prices. We shall be examining this in more detail in Chapter 3.

WHO PAYS THE BETTING TAX?

With effect from 1 January 2002, there is no duty payable to Customs & Excise on financial spread bets placed with bookmakers. The duty has been replaced by a tax levied by the Treasury on the net losses of their clients.

The bookmaker is responsible for the accounting and payment of this tax and so you do not have to make any provision for this liability.

This whole question is subject to change in legislation.

⟶ Summary

In this chapter we have:

- described a financial spread bet in detail;
- demonstrated with worked examples how the bet can be used both for rising and falling share or index prices;
- examined the effects of gearing, with the consequent increase in both the potential benefits as well as the degree of risk; and
- defined the spread and what it includes, such as the government betting tax and the bookmaker's turn.

3

Types of financial spread bet

Intraday bets

Futures based bets

Notional trading requirements

Margin calls

Running more than one bet simultaneously

Why use financial spread bets?

What can you bet on?

What you can expect from your bookmaker

What your bookmaker expects from you

In this chapter we discuss in detail the two different types of financial spread bet that are on offer. These are:

- intraday bets
- futures based bets, or underlying market based bets.

The chapter also discusses:

- notional trading requirements, or bet size factors
- margin calls
- possible reasons for using financial spread bets
- what you can expect from your bookmaker
- what your bookmaker can expect from you.

To the purist, it may seem misleading to label one type of very short term bet 'intraday', and another one 'futures based', since the quotations that the financial bookmaker will make to you are both based on a futures price. However, we have adopted this method to differentiate between bets that have a life that is limited to one market session, and bets which can have a much longer life before they have to be closed out.

INTRADAY BETS

An intraday bet has a life which starts and ends during market hours for the day in which the bet is placed or it can start after the close of business on the previous working day. For example, an intraday bet placed on the FTSE 100 Index can be placed at any time from 1631 hours on, say Monday, until the London market shuts at 1630 hours on Tuesday. You may well be able to place a bet on-line at any hour of the day or night, in or out of market hours, but

> ...it remains best practice to deal only during market hours...

you will not necessarily get the best spread price at 00.01, for example, if there is only one bookmaker offering an on-line facility at that time. We believe that it remains best practice to deal only during market hours when you are presented with the widest possible choice of live spread prices.

Depending upon the market you are contemplating, you can open the bet at any time during that period, and you can close it at any time during the same period or, you can let the bet run on until it is closed automatically at the end of the trading period. If you leave the bet to 'die' at the end of the day, you must be aware that as far as the FTSE 100 is concerned, the market price will be subject to an adjustment between 1630 hours and approximately 1640 hours each day, and the final figure can be substantially higher or lower than it was at 1629 hours. Sometimes this adjustment can add considerably to your winnings; sometimes it can exacerbate a loss. Sometimes it can turn a small win into a loss, or a small loss into a win. The adjustment is known as the 'auction' and it happens as a result of daily limit orders for individual shares being unwound or cancelled in the stock market. There is no way of anticipating which way the adjustment will push the Index, nor can you estimate the extent of the move.

You can place similar bets on other indices during their market hours, such as the Dow Jones Industrial Average, the Nasdaq, or the Standard & Poors 500 in New York, or the CAC in France, the DAX in Germany or the Hang Seng in Hong Kong. Intraday bets are very popular and widely used for many reasons. They account for about 50 per cent of all bets traded daily.

In Chapter 2, I explained that when the bookmaker quotes you a spread price, it is valid at the time that the quotation is made. The reason why the quotation may not be available at exactly the same price one minute later is because of the volatility in share and index prices in the stock market. On one hand, you want the prices to move because you have more of a chance of making worthwhile winnings if the price movement is substantial. On the other hand, considerable volatility demands that you watch the movement of the prices quoted and get regular price feeds so that you can close the bet to minimize any loss if the market moves against you. The only way to monitor the price movement properly is to use a PC together with a suitable software program. The best one that I have come across which represents good value for money is Updata Trader Professional. Alternatively, you might care to join the Internet Sporting Club Ltd who, for a fee, will provide you with a pager giving you a real time price record of the FTSE 100 Index, updated every 30 seconds automatically, and who advise you when to open and when to close an intraday bet. In addition, they will advise on futures based bets on individual shares in the same way (see Appendix 2).

FUTURES BASED BETS

A futures based bet is based on the price of the index or individual share price quoted for the next quarter day, or the one after that, and it runs from the time that the bet is contracted until the future quarter day, when it dies. Although the date on which the bet dies is referred to as a quarter day, the actual date will not necessarily be the 25th day of January, March, September or December. The date will vary from about the 18th to the 22nd of those months. The actual dates are published on the web pages of each spread betting bookmaker. However, you can close it at any time you want – even ten minutes after opening it, if that suits you. In the example of a telephoned price enquiry and instruction to open a bet shown in Chapter 4, the client asks for the price of the FTSE Futures, and the dealer asks which ones are required for the quote. They ask 'June or September?' The reason is that the futures market trades to the quarter days and as

> .... **the futures market trades to the quarter days** ....

a rule of thumb, these are often the third Wednesday of each quarter (June, September, December and March) every year. Futures contracts expire on or close to the quarter days.

Suppose that it is the beginning of November, and the share in question is Shell. You think that the share price will move up, for a variety of reasons. You ask for the price of Shell futures, and you have to choose between December (being the next quarter day) and March.

The decision as to which one you select will be influenced by the reasons for your belief that the price of Shell will rise. For example, you may have read in newspapers or investment magazines that a bid for the company is expected to be announced in the next few days, or you have reason to believe that the company is about to announce that it has discovered a major new oil field. In that case you would expect an immediate uplift in the price (or downturn, depending on the reasons for your anticipation of the direction the share price will take), and so you might well decide to take the December quarter day price. If, however, you are basing your expectations for the price movement on such items as an increase/decrease in the oil supply quotas, as agreed by OPEC, for example, or an increase/decrease in the price per barrel because of a very cold (or mild) winter, then you would probably elect to base your bet on the next quarter day but one, i.e. March, in this example, because it might take longer than 25 December for the market to react to the news, and you do not want the bet to die on you just before you start to show some substantial winnings.

In many ways it is identical to an intraday bet, but there are some important differences.

NOTIONAL TRADING REQUIREMENTS

When you decide to make a bet, the bookmaker will want to ensure that you have enough cash in your account with him to cover any potential losses that might occur if the underlying futures price moves against you, even if only temporarily. The sum of money that is required is called the notional trading requirement (NTR). Some bookmakers call it the Bet Size Factor. It is calculated by taking into account the amount of your intended stake and the known volatility of the instrument on which you want to bet. For example, if you want to commit a stake of £5 per point on the FTSE 100 for a futures based bet, the calculation to arrive at the amount of NTR could be 300 x £5 = £1500. In some cases the multiplication factor might be less, and in some cases it might be more. It is very important that you understand that this requirement exists, particularly when you have several open positions running at the same time. Each bookmaker will supply you with a table of NTR multiplication factors when you ask to be advised of their terms and conditions. In this book the factors for different instruments are shown in Appendix 1 and they are to be found under the column headed 'Bet size factor'.

MARGIN CALLS

In addition to the requirement to deposit funds to cover the NTR when you open a bet, it is quite possible that there will be margin calls if you place a futures based bet and let it run for more than one day. The worked example below illustrates how and why this financial demand occurs.

✱ EXAMPLE

You have deposited £2000 (the NTR) with your bookmaker. Let us suppose that it is 4 February and you want to place the bet on the futures price of Vodafone Airtouch for the March quarter day.

You telephone the bookmaker and he makes a price to you of 234p bid, 237p offered. You decide to 'buy' the share because you believe that the price will go up, and so you elect to bet at £10 per penny and you buy at 237p.

At the close of business the next day, 5 February, the price moves against you and drops 50p to 184p bid, 187p offered. The bookmaker has to 'settle' the loss with the market by 5pm that day.

Your account will now be £500 in debit (50 pence x £10 = £500). The bookmaker asks you to deposit a further £500 with him in order to maintain your deposit (NTR), or cushion, at the minimum level required of £2000. This is called a cash call, and if the price drops further you will be asked for more calls until the price turns upwards.

A week later, at the close of business on 11 February, the price of Vodafone rises by 25 pence to 209p bid, 212p offered. Your bookmaker will 'settle' the profit by obtaining a cash payment of £250 (25 pence x £10 = £250).

Your account will be credited with £250 on that day. You can either leave this sum with the bookmaker, or ask him to refund it to you. You may be able to leave it 'in the kitty' so to speak, and arrange for it to earn interest on a daily basis along with the minimum deposit. You have to ask the bookmaker to provide this facility, and it pays to raise this question when you shop around initially, to make your choice of bookmaker.

The following week, on 18 February, the price climbs again, back to 234p bid, 237p offered. You obtain a further refund of £250, which completes the repayment of the balance of the £500 cash call that you had to make when the price had dropped.

The following week, on 25 February, the price rises to 298p bid, 301p offered. You decide to watch the progress.

On 4 March, the price falls back to 277p bid, 280p offered, and you decide to close out the bargain. You sell to close at 277p and your profit on your original bet is £400 (Sold @ 277p – Bought @ 237p = 40 pence x £10 per penny = £400).

You may ask 'What happens to the call money?'

When the price moved against you from the original opening bet level of 237p, you had to pay a call of £500. This money was refunded during the time that the bet was running when the price had returned to the opening level. Thereafter, when your bet had started to show a profit, there were no calls made. It does not matter how high your 'paper' profit gets, there will not be any more cash demands whilst you are in profit.

This daily settlement procedure will continue while the bet is open. It makes no difference whether your bet is to buy, or to short sell an index or an individual share. If, at the end of each day, the 'settlement price' of any bet you have which is open puts your account in debit, you will be asked to put up more margin. If, however, at the end of each day the settlement price puts your account into credit, you will receive funds into your account equal to that amount. Your bookmaker is not in

> This daily settlement procedure continues while the bet is open

the business of lending money, but part of the service he must provide is the daily administration of the settlement system on your behalf.

The same procedure applies in reverse if you had decided originally that the share price was going to fall, and you had 'sold' (or gone short) of Vodafone Airtouch when you opened the bet. Cash calls would be initiated if the share price had risen, and refunds payable if it had fallen back subsequently, until you had closed out the bet.

RUNNING MORE THAN ONE BET SIMULTANEOUSLY

It is possible to run more than one bet simultaneously, on different shares, and at different future closing dates. Thus, you could have a 'buy' open for one share, whilst simultaneously running a 'sell' bet for another share, and both bets could have different expiry dates.

Most financial bookmakers refuse to accept simultaneous buy and sell bets for the same share or index. You will find this exclusion published in their list of terms and conditions.

You can close out all or part of a bet at any time you like before the expiry date. The expiry date is the date when the 'future' on which the bet is based, dies. It may be, for example, that you have two different 'buy' bets running simultaneously, and both are showing substantial profits, but you think there is more to go. You decide to open another bet on a third share. In order to avoid sending more cash to your account to cover the extra NTR for the new bet, you might close out some of each of the first two to release a proportion of the profits and apply those funds to cover the extra cash requirement.

WHY USE FINANCIAL SPREAD BETS?

There are several very good reasons for using financial spread bets.

First, they are a very useful short term insurance, or hedge, if you think something might happen that could affect your existing shareholding.

Assume that you have a share in your portfolio that is showing a substantial profit over your purchase price, and you think that the price could fall substantially in the short term. You do not want to sell the share because you would be creating a significant liability to CGT if you dispose of the holding, whilst at the same time you do not want to miss out on the intrinsic profit at

> **Financial spread bets are a very useful short term insurance**

the current price. A good example of this situation could be when other companies within the sector in which your holding sits, start issuing profit warnings when they report their interim or year end figures. You then expect the market to mark down the expected earnings target for the company whose shares you hold, with a consequent substantial mark down of the share price. This happened in the clothes retail sector in 2001, and the price of Matalan fell by 50 per cent in the space of a few minutes. The fall was totally unreasonable, as is often the case, and the price recovered somewhat during the rest of the day, but the damage had been massive and swift. Spread betting would have allowed you to do several things.

First, it would have allowed you to protect your holding against loss.

■ You could have placed a bet to 'short sell' another share in the same sector that you believed might fall when that company reported, even if you did not hold the share. There could well be a chance of a profit if the market reacted as strongly.

■ You could have placed a bet to buy the share (in this case Matalan), when you saw the extent of the fall in the share price, on the basis that the market always overreacts when unexpected news comes out of the blue. You would have been able to make a profit in a few minutes in that case, but you would have had to be quick. This is a good example of the need for real time prices and the ability to watch the market all the time.

Second, it enables you to deal in much greater quantities of individual shares or indices because of the substantial amount of gearing attached to spread betting. The average is about 14 times, and the capital required to spread bet is modest compared with Contracts for Difference (CFDs), an alternative instrument, which is examined in Chapter 5.

Third, and just as important as the other two reasons, financial spread betting allows you to short sell a share, which the current system of settlement inhibits to such an extent, for all practical purposes, that it is well nigh impossible to execute.

WHAT CAN YOU BET ON?

A full list of the instruments on which you can bet is shown in Appendix 1. They range over market indices such as the FTSE (London), the Dow Jones (USA), the Hang Seng (Hong Kong), the Dax (Frankfurt) and the CAC (Paris), as well as all the futures and options that are traded including oil, metals, commodities, utilities and bonds globally.

It is important to know the terms and conditions offered and operated by whichever spread-betting bookmaker with whom you decide to open an account, because there are variations between each one. One condition that you must know, is the date on which futures based contracts expire. Another essential issue to consider is the different spreads that apply if you impose stop loss limits, and the amount of any additional widening of the spread if the stop loss is guaranteed. These issues are examined in detail in Chapter 4.

WHAT CAN YOU EXPECT FROM YOUR BOOKMAKER

When you decide to open an account with one or more financial bookmakers, there are several areas concerning your rights and obligations that you should be aware of. It is essential that you understand the terms and conditions of business of the firm with which you are proposing to deal, so that there are no unpleasant surprises awaiting you after you have committed yourself financially.

There are several things you can expect from your financial bookmaker relating to the conduct of your account and more general business practices.

Fast execution-only service

If one is to draw a comparison with conventional dealing and investment in stocks and shares, the role of a financial bookmaker is more akin to that of a market maker, rather than that of a stockbroker. Financial bookmakers do not give you advice on whether or not to bet, nor on which way to bet (up or down), nor on what index or share to bet on. They have exactly the same role as that of turf accountants at a racecourse, or in a betting shop. After all, you would not expect to get tips at a race meeting from the bookies.

However, bookmakers are acting as principals, and as far as clients are concerned, they do not have to 'go to the market' to place their orders consequent upon receiving instructions. They make their prices to clients there and then, and the client either places a bet or declines to do anything. In this respect, making an investment

> Speed can lead to misunderstanding

commitment with a financial bookmaker is much quicker than buying or selling a share using a stockbroker, other than via an on-line dealing service.

What you can expect is rapid service. Don't forget that there may be many telephone lines ringing in the bookmaker's office so they want to get your business placed as quickly as possible and get on with the next client. Speed can lead to misunderstanding and it is because of this danger that it is essential that you give your instructions clearly and concisely, and that you get the bookmaker to repeat them back to you both at the time that you open and when you close out a bet.

In order to give you instant quotations for all the instruments on which it is possible to bet, the bookmaker must have immediate access to a mass of current market data. Volatile markets mean constantly changing prices. Such a vast array of market information demands a sophisticated and efficient electronic system both for obtaining quotations and laying off bets in the market. You should never be asked to wait for more than a few seconds for a price quotation. The trend, nowadays, is for more and more bookmakers to offer on-line dealing facilities. This minimizes the time it takes to place a bet.

It should, however, be noted that, usually, it is not possible to place bets on-line with a guaranteed stop-loss.

Contract notes and statements service

The bookmaker must send you a contract note for every bet that you place and the contract note must be posted or sent by e-mail on the same day that the transaction is executed. A statement should be sent to you once a week. This should show the amount of cash that is held to your credit as well as details of any interest earned or dividends received. It should also record details of executed bets, including the amounts of any stakes and current liabilities, such as any dividend claims due to the market, or additional margin requirements payable.

If there are any errors, or figures with which you disagree, you must contact the bookmaker immediately on receipt of the contract note or statement.

It will create considerable extra administrative work and consequent delay in sorting out the facts of a case when a disagreement arises, if several days elapse between the objection being raised and the date and time of the event in question.

WHAT YOUR BOOKMAKER EXPECTS FROM YOU

Above all else, your bookmakers expect you to keep sufficient liquid funds in your accounts so they can meet any daily obligations they may have in settling their position with the market. Clearly, since the futures prices can be very volatile from one day to another, they will want to hold sufficient funds to give them a cushion, or margin of safety, so that they have time to call up more money from you if the bet is to remain open, although the price of the underlying security is moving in the wrong direction from your point of view. If they have not got enough funds available, they will close the bet, if they can, before the position gets into debit.

Summary

In this chapter we have discussed the difference between the two different types of spread bet, as well as the capital requirements you will need to make available. The main items we have examined are:

- intraday bets being those with a life limited to the duration of a daily market, which die, or are automatically closed out at the end of the session, unless you have given instructions to close the bet before the market shuts for the day;

- futures based bets which you may want to let run for days or weeks before the date on which the underlying future ceases to exist, which will be a quarter day some time ahead;

- the ways to calculate the amount of cash to be deposited before you make a particular bet to satisfy the notional trading requirement, or bet size factor, and how these sums may vary substantially depending upon the instrument that you choose on which to bet;

- the need to make provision for margin calls which may be required whilst the bet is open;

- the different reasons for using financial spread betting;
- what you can expect from your bookmaker; and
- what your bookmaker can expect from you.

4

Instructing your dealer

In this chapter we describe the vital need for unequivocal and concise instructions to protect yourself against expensive misunderstandings when:

- opening a bet
- closing a bet
- imposing a stop loss limit
- closing or removing a stop loss limit
- setting a limit order.

HOW TO PLACE YOUR BET

Most financial spread bets are placed over the telephone. Although technological progress has been rapid, and huge progress has been made in communication systems, there is still room for mistakes and misunderstandings to occur. Since you are committing your capital to risk whenever you bet, it is essential that the person who is executing your instructions in the bookmaker's office understands completely what it is that you wish to do. You may think that it is unnecessary to describe the procedure to be used in such detail, but rest assured that it will save you much argument and possible unpleasantness if you follow these guidelines when you place a financial spread bet.

OPENING A BET

Here is a typical conversation between you, the investor, and the dealer in the bookmaker firm (D = Dealer; C = Client):

D:	Good afternoon 'Bookmaker', Matt speaking.
C:	Hi Matt, can I have your price for FTSE Futures, please?
D:	What period would you like, June or September?
C:	Oh, June please.
D:	OK one moment please.
D: [*to trader*]	*June FTSE please [the price is repeated back to the bet taker].*
D:	June FTSE is 6600 at 6608 (six six zero zero at six six zero eight).*
C:	OK, I think it will go higher so I should like to buy at £10 a point at 6608 please.
D: [*to trader*]	*You lose ten pounds of the June FTSE at 6608.*

D:	OK, to confirm, you buy £10 of June FTSE at 6608. Could I take your account number please?
C:	It's BOJ 007.
D:	Thank you, and your name please?
C:	The name's Bond … James Bond.
D:	OK, Mr Bond, was that an opening or closing trade?
C:	What do you mean by opening or closing trade?
D:	If it's a new trade, then it is 'to open', but if it is closing an existing position, then it is 'to close'.
C:	OK, then that's an opening trade.
D:	OK, just to confirm the details with you: **You bought £10 of the June FTSE at 6608 to open.**
C:	Yes, that is correct.
D:	Thank you for your business, sir, and good luck.
C:	Thank you, goodbye.

This rather boring record of a telephone conversation illustrates some very important points. Let us start with the item which is marked *.

In every firm of financial bookmakers there is at least one individual, called the trader in this conversation, who is responsible for 'laying the odds', or making the price and spread. All the dealers have to refer to the trader for a price every time an investor asks for one. When the prices in the particular market in question, or that of an individual share or index is moving rapidly, it is called a fast market. The indices such as the FTSE 100, the Dow Jones Industrial Average, the Nasdaq and the Hang Seng are notorious for their intraday volatility. Conse-

> **it is essential that you make your decision fast**

quently, in order to protect themselves against loss when they wish to lay off your bet in the futures market, the traders will only maintain their 'quotation' for a very short time. You will not be able to go away and think about it. Nor will you be able to prolong your discussion with the dealer whilst you consider whether or not to place a bet, and expect the price quoted to remain the same. Thus, it is essential that you make your decision fast when you have been given the prices.

Even when firms have introduced on-line trading facilities, the final acceptance of the price of a bet rests with the bookmaker, and you can only be sure that your bet has been agreed when you receive proper confirmation, whether on-line or verbally, as illustrated in that part of the conversation shown above in bold letters. When your bet has been accepted, the bookmaker will lay it off elsewhere to protect himself. This process is described in Chapter 5.

THE VITAL NEED FOR PRECISE INSTRUCTIONS

Remember that all telephone conversations with financial spread betting bookmakers are taped. This means that if you ever have a dispute after you have placed a bet, you are entitled to ask to hear the tape recording of the relevant conversation, so that both sides can hear again the exact words used by both parties at the time. There are occasions when the clarity of speech can be obscured by interference or background noise, so it is in your interests that these conversations should be taped.

CONFIRMATION OF YOUR INSTRUCTIONS

It is essential that the instructions are repeated at least twice in order to minimize any possibility of misunderstanding. The importance of this point will be reinforced when we discuss the question of imposing a stop loss limit to curtail any potential loss if the price goes against you while the bet is open.

STOP LOSS LIMITS

We have shown how volatile the market can be, and we have explained that you need to have both volatility and momentum to make the greatest profit when spread betting intraday on market indices. The corollary to that situation is, of course, that such large movements in an index or individual share price will increase the risk of loss. The most dangerous situation arises if you have 'gone short', i.e. 'sold' a market or share, and the market turns against you. Under these conditions, there is *no limit* to the amount you could lose.

✳ EXAMPLE

Assume that you decide that the share price of XYZ plc is going to take a nosedive because the political or economic climate is changing rapidly for the worse, or perhaps you think that war will be declared in the part of the world that is vital to the company. Further, let us assume that the share price is currently 500p bid (to sell), and 501p offered (to buy).

- Suppose you bought the share and the company went bust. You would lose 500p per share. Suppose you were prepared to invest £5000, which for ease of illustration we shall assume buys you 1000 shares. You would know before you dealt, that the maximum you could lose would be £5000.

- Suppose you 'sold short' 1000 shares at 500p per share, in the expectation of buying them back in a short time at say, 200p per share. All your fears turn out to be groundless. There is no war, and the company reports record earnings with a lot more to come. The world at large buys heavily because they have decided that this is the share to hold. The share price could keep on going up and up. You have contracted to deliver 1000 shares to the market within a specific period on settlement day, and you have got to buy them before that date in order to honour your commitment. At the time that you entered into the contract there was no way that you could have predicted or quantified the extent of your potential loss.

- The effect of gearing, which we explain later on, can exacerbate this risk substantially. If you are making intraday bets, as opposed to a futures based one, the downside risk may be somewhat less, but even so, with the FTSE 100 and Dow Jones indices having demonstrated very large one-day movements, you are well advised to impose stop loss limits when you open your bets.

When you place the bet to open, after you have asked the price of the instrument upon which you wish to place your bet, you should say 'I buy/sell the [FTSE 100, or whatever you have chosen] at £10 per point with a guaranteed stop loss of XX points'. You must ensure that when the dealer repeats the details of your bet back to you, they include the words 'guaranteed stop loss', as well as the number of points that you have stipulated. There are two types of stop loss. Ordinary stop loss, and guaranteed stop loss. If the market is moving against you in a gradual manner, and you have demanded the imposition of an ordinary stop loss, there is a good chance that the dealer in the financial bookmaker will remember your instructions and close out your bet at, or very close to the figure that you have agreed as the stop loss limit. *However, in a fast market, this closing bet is not guaranteed.* It is precisely under these fast market conditions that the need of the protection of a stop loss is the greatest, so you are strongly advised to choose a guaranteed stop loss limit. Then, however fast the market moves against you, the full extent of your liability will be limited if the bet goes wrong. It will stop an acceptable loss becoming a disaster.

Suppose, for example, that your stake is £10 per point in the case of an index based bet, or £10 per 1 penny in the case of a futures based bet on an individual share and you place an ordinary stop loss limit on a bet where you buy to open. The price of the index could drop 150 points in a few seconds if there were some disastrous economic news, or 300p if there were to be an unexpected profits warning, and you would have incurred heavy losses, which could have been avoided.

CLOSING A BET

To close a bet that is running, you adopt the same procedure as when you open a bet, but the instruction to buy or sell is the opposite to that which you gave when you opened the bet. The simple way to explain what to do is to regard a bet as being synonymous with a share or unit trust. There is a 'bid' price and there is an 'offer' price. Whichever you started (opened) with, requires you do the opposite when you want to stop (close). *You do not have to close out the whole bet if you don't want to do so.*

If you do not close out the whole bet, you must remember that you still have a bet running and that your capital is still at risk.

REMOVAL OF STOP LOSS LIMITS

The question whether the bet is 'opening' or 'closing' has great significance.

✱ EXAMPLE

Let us assume that you want to place a bet at £10 per point to buy the FTSE 100 index at 6608 to open, as described in the conversation above, but at the same time you want to limit your liability to catastrophic loss if the index turns down against you.

You stipulate a guaranteed stop loss limit of 40 points which would incur a debt of £400 if the index falls out of bed, and you make sure that the dealer confirms the limit by repeating it back to you.

The market moves in the right direction for you, and the index climbs 33 points. Then it stops going up and starts to go sideways for a bit, before starting to fall slowly. You decide to close out your bet whilst you can lock in a profit of 30 points before it goes down any further, and so you telephone the bookmaker. The chances are that you connect with a different dealer from the one who took your opening bet. You must go through the following routine:

- Ask for the price of the instrument whose opening bet you want to close. In this case you would ask for the price of the June FTSE, which you *bought* for the opening bet.
- If the bid price is acceptable (which is the only one in which you are interested in this example), you say 'I sell the June FTSE at, say, 6638 *to close my previous bet*'.

■ You *must* also say 'please remove the guaranteed stop loss limit of 40 points that I requested when I placed the opening bet'.

■ If you are only closing a part of the opening bet, you *must* confirm the removal of the guaranteed stop loss limit of the part that you are closing *and* you must confirm that the remainder that is left running continues to be protected by the stop loss.

■ If you finally close out the remainder of the bet, you *must* confirm the removal of the guaranteed stop loss limit that is still open.

■ There is no need to remove the guaranteed stop loss limit for an intraday bet if you leave the bet running until the market closes. The bet will be closed automatically at the final official figure (cash) at which the market closed, and because your liability ceases at that time and bet 'dies' officially, the guaranteed stop loss limit will die with it.

You may ask why it is so important to be so specific about:

■ asking for the price of the instrument included in the opening bet; and

■ removing a stop loss limit.

The reason why you must ask for the specific instrument concerned with your opening bet, in this case the June FTSE, is because you may have several opening bets running at the same time and it is necessary to identify the one that you want to close out. It is not sufficient simply to refer 'to my earlier bet', particularly if some time has elapsed since your opening bet, even if you have only got one position running. Also, you may have opened a 'buy' on the June FTSE, and a 'sell' on the September FTSE, for example.

Unfortunately computers do not think, or link opening and closing instructions to stop loss limits, which may or may not exist in conjunction with those orders. Just let us look at what can happen.

You place an opening 'buy' bet together with a stop loss limit, and subsequently you 'sell' to close the opening bet, and you have made a profit. In this example you would have won:

30 (points) x £10 = £300.

Subsequently the FTSE 100 index falls like a stone, perhaps because there has been some bad economic news from the USA for example, and it drops to 6598. The computer will have been instructed to sell your opening contract, in this case, unless the programmed instruction is removed at the time that you closed the bet. It will not necessarily be removed unless you give the requisite instructions, and you could find that you have incurred a loss of 40 (points) x £10 = £400, which would more than wipe out your win!

The exercise of a stop loss limit applies to a contract to 'sell to open' in exactly the same way as one to 'buy to open', as explained above.

It is very easy to forget that you imposed a stop loss limit when the bet is running strongly in your favour. You become so excited at working out your winnings that when you close out the bet, you overlook the fact that you placed such a limit at the opening. This is particularly true when you are making intraday bets because the time span between opening and closing is very often only a few minutes.

LIMIT ORDERS

A limit order is not to be confused with a stop loss limit. In fact, a limit order it is the opposite of a stop loss limit because you want to use it to lock in a profit. Let us look at an example.

The graph of the FTSE 100 index shown in Fig 4.1 demonstrates a typical start to the day. By 0900 every working day the market makers have opened their quotes and all the shares listed in the FTSE 100 have been loaded with firm purchase and sale limit orders on the market. You look at the chart and decide to place an opening bet to buy the index at 5928 because you think that the market is going to go up. For the purpose of this example we shall ignore the spreads and the difference between the cash price and the bookmaker's quotation based on a futures price. You place a guaranteed *stop loss* limit of, say, 40 points below your opening price, at 5888, to limit your potential downside loss, and you place a *limit* order at, say, 5936 to close out the bet. That means that if the price goes above 5936, *and then falls back*, you have locked in the difference between

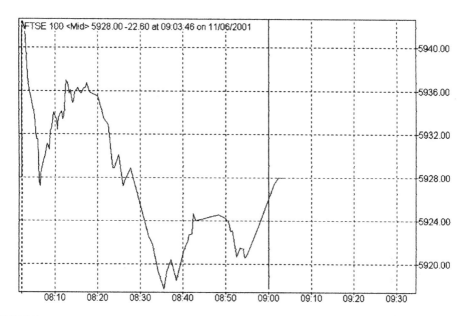

FTSE 100 <Mid> 5928.00 -22.60 at 09:03.46 on 11/06/2001

FIG 4.1 FTSE 100 index at start of the day

the opening bet and the limit that you have set. Thus, you would be assured of a win of 8 points, whatever happens to the index subsequently.

In fact the index reached a high of 5490 before retreating to 5931 at around 0940 (see Fig 4.2), so your limit order would have been activated at 5936.

Note that the imposition of both stop loss limits and limit orders may cause the bookmaker to widen the spread substantially, so you need to take this into consideration when you are deciding whether or not to impose such limits. Unless there is sufficient movement in the price, you may find that it is not worthwhile to place limit orders. You should always protect yourself by imposing stop loss limits.

Figure 4.3 shows what actually happened that day, and demonstrates clearly the importance of stop loss limits. Your opening bet was a 'buy', at 5928, and the index closed at 5864. The difference is 64 points, which, at £10 per point represents a loss of £640. It was avoidable.

It is to your advantage if you discipline yourself to write down in a diary, or betting record book *all* the details of your bets and refer to your notes when you open or close a bet.

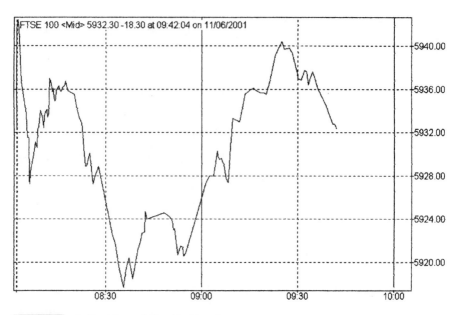

FIG 4.2 Activation of the limit order

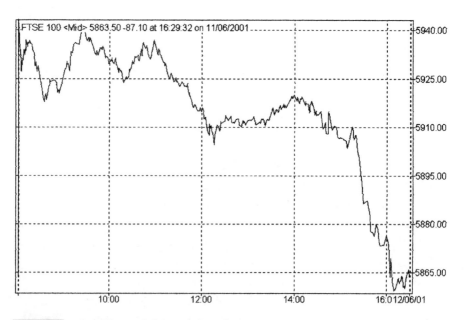

FIG 4.3 The effect of the stop loss limit

THE LEGAL POSITION

Any debt that has arisen as a direct result of placing a financial spread bet in the UK is recoverable at court under current legislation. There is a popular myth that one can walk away from any financial obligation to a bookmaker because a bet is treated differently from any other transaction. This is not true.

When you place a bet with a financial bookmaker, you enter into a contract in just the same way as when you give instructions to your stockbroker, or bank, to buy or sell securities on your behalf. The fact that the very nature of the business does not allow enough time to complete a written contract does not matter one jot. A verbal contract is as binding as a written one, and the financial bookmakers will use all the legal powers that are available to recover any debt due to them.

> **A verbal contract is as binding as a written one**

The protection covers both parties to the transaction, and you have similar recourse to the courts and the same protection if you believe that there are grounds to recover monies due to you consequent upon any financial spread bets that you have placed with a licensed financial bookmaker.

Clearly, no one wants to become involved in any litigation, which is expensive and time consuming. Thus, you will understand how important it is to ensure that you give unequivocal and very clear instructions when you open or close a bet.

HOW THE BOOKMAKER LAYS OFF YOUR BET

Theoretically, there are only three ways that bookmakers can limit their exposure to risk from bets they have accepted.

They can attempt to lay off bets with other bookmakers, possibly at a price that is marginally different, but to their advantage. This is almost impossible to do in practical terms.

They can run their own books and carry the risks themselves by hoping to match 'buys' with 'sells'. They would have to vary the prices that they quote to attract more buyers than sellers if there were more bets laid on the downside in order to bring the books back to a more level position, and vice versa. This is a dangerous practice but it is not unknown. The trouble is that doing so may result in the prices offered by one bookmaker becoming so much out of line with those offered by others that it opens the door to arbitrageurs. It is quite normal to find a variation in the prices on offer of a couple of pence, perhaps, for the same index or share, but if the spread becomes substantially different from the others, you can place a 'buy' bet with one bookmaker and a 'sell' bet with another simultaneously, making an immediate profit without incurring any risk whatsoever.

The normal practice is to lay off the bet by purchasing a Contract For Difference (CFD) immediately the bet has been accepted. Thus, the bookmaker generally takes no risk whatsoever and their 'turn', or commission, as well as the betting tax, is embodied in the difference in the spread between their price to you and the cost to them of the CFD. It means that their margin of profit is fairly thin, so they need a continuous flow and a high volume of bets to earn a living.

This ability to lay off bets and reduce their exposure to loss means that the financial bookmaker cannot lose money in any significant amounts, unlike the ordinary turf accountant on the racecourse. It has one other unique advantage. The financial bookmaker's firm is only too pleased to broadcast and acclaim the occasions when people make big wins through his agency, since that is the best way to attract other clients to the firm. Another spin off from this way of controlling risk is that you are most unlikely to be asked to place your business elsewhere as a result of a consistent record of winning bets.

Summary

In this chapter we have emphasized the need for you to protect yourself from potentially expensive misunderstandings, by making sure that your instructions to the dealer are absolutely clear. We have described:

- the need to ensure that the dealer understands the buy or sell order, together with the date of the future on which your bet is to be placed, as well as the amount of the stake and imposition, if any, of the stop loss limit;

- the importance of making sure that the dealer links your order to close a bet with the correct open one;

- the essential specific separate instruction to remove any applicable stop loss limit that may be linked to your closing bet instructions, and the corresponding dangers that can arise if you omit to give these specific instructions; and

- how the bookmaker lays off his risk when he accepts a bet from a client.

5

Contracts for Difference

What is a Contract for Difference?

Universal Stock Futures (USFs) compared with Contracts for Difference

In this chapter we describe the investment instrument known as a Contract for Difference (CFD). In particular we explain:

- what are Contracts for Difference
- how they are geared
- their uses and applications
- dividend treatment
- tax treatment
- comparisons of cost between investing in a Contract for Difference and a financial spread bet.

WHAT IS A CONTRACT FOR DIFFERENCE?

A CFD can be described as a tradable instrument that is based on an individual share. The CFD trades on margin allowing the trader to enjoy a considerable amount of gearing. It can be used to trade long or short of stock to mirror the performance of the underlying share.

Trading in CFDs is usually carried out only by experienced investors or professional traders. It can be dangerous for inexperienced or occasional investors.

Trading on margin, or margin trading as it is more often called, allows you to buy or sell shares without having to put up the full price at the time that you execute the bargain. The number of shares in which you can trade will depend upon the margin requirement demanded by the bookmaker, and typically this percentage will vary between 10 and 25 per cent, depending on the share and the country of residence of the client, i.e. you.

Gearing

Suppose you deposit £20,000 with the bookmaker. You want to buy a share because you think that the price will go up. Let us assume that the market price is 498p bid, and 500p offered. Let us assume that the share in question falls into the 10 per cent margin requirement category.

You would be able to buy 40,000 shares using a CFD. If you had to pay for the shares outright at the time of purchase, you would only have been able to buy 4000 shares. So you can see that the gearing is substantial.

The amount of the margin requirement will depend to a large extent on the volatility in the price of the share in question, as well as the size of the market capitalization of the company concerned. If, after you have dealt in the CFD the underlying price moves against you, the bookmaker will call for additional funds to be deposited with them to maintain the differential between the share price and the deposit. *Remember that the margin requirement is calculated on the full contract value, and that includes costs.*

The uses and applications of CFDs

CFDs can be used in exactly the same way as financial spread bets, but they have some significant differences and benefits, particularly with regard to their 'lifetime', and their participation in dividends payable by the underlying company on which the contract is based. The capital requirement, especially the amount of NTR, is substantially higher and consequently, the amounts of capital that need to be available for this type of investment are greater. Generally they appeal to those with substantial sums of money to invest, as well as institutional fund and investment managers.

> the margin requirement is calculated on the full contract value

Trading short as well as long

Trading short means selling something that you do not possess. In the past, before the introduction of the electronic settlement system, you could sell stock that you did not own during the Stock Exchange accounting period (usually 14 days), and buy it back before the end of the period. If the price of the share had dropped between the date on which you bought the share and the date on which you closed out your 'sold' position, you received a cheque for the difference on settlement day. However, if the price had gone against you, you paid the difference.

Now, the imposition of rolling settlement means that every day is a complete trading period on its own. This has effectively abolished this form of trading on credit other than for periods ranging from intraday to one week and the chances of substantial share price movement generally within this restricted period are considerably reduced. The ability to roll positions over from one accounting period to another are fast disappearing, quite apart from the unattractive dealing costs that can apply.

Since there is no expiry date for a CFD, this instrument has become very attractive indeed to people who want to trade the price downwards.

Trading long is self explanatory. It is the opposite of short selling, and it means buying something, usually a stock, a share or a future. The attraction of this method employing CFDs lies in the gearing. It enables you to deal in far greater quantities of the share without having to fund the outright purchase.

Hedging a risk

Trading CFDs enables you to protect the inherent profit in a share holding, should you believe that the price is due for a short term correction downwards. It may be beneficial to follow this route to control the liability to CGT. *Remember, this action does <u>not</u> have the same potential liabilities that are associated with writing call traded options.*

Cost effective

No government stamp duty is incurred when you trade a CFD. Usually brokers' commissions are lower than those charged for conventional share dealing.

Dividends

A holder of a CFD is entitled to 80 per cent of the gross dividend. The reason is because the creation of a CFD is based upon the physical purchase or sale of the underlying shares in the quantity that is denominated in the CFD. If you bought 40,000 shares as shown in the example above, the firm that issues the CFD to you actually enters into a contract to buy the shares outright, even though you only pay down a small percentage of the overall cost. If, therefore, during the life of the CFD there is a dividend receivable to the holder of those shares, you will be entitled to a large part of that payment.

On the other hand, if you have sold shares short within the CFD, and there is a dividend payable during the life of that CFD, you will be liable to pay 100 per cent to the market of the gross dividend receivable.

Expiry

You can hold your long or short positions for as long as you like. A CFD has no settlement date. It is an open ended contract. All it will cost you during that period is the cost of financing a long position, apart from any loss incurred between the opening and closing prices at the termination of the contract.

Financing

The bookmaker will charge you for the cost of borrowing the money needed to fund the purchase of the underlying shares for a long position. This charge will be calculated on a *per diem* basis and is applicable for any long position overnight starting from the close of business on the day that you open the bargain. The charge is based on a percentage increase above the current London Inter Bank Offered Rate (LIBOR). It does not apply to intraday trading.

> A CFD is an open ended contract

In just the same way, you will be credited with a rebate for any short positions held within a CFD instrument daily after the first trading period. The rebate is based on a percentage below the current London Inter Bank Interest Discount Rate (LIBID).

Commission

A small commission charge is made each time a contract is opened or closed. This is typically about 0.25 per cent. You may ask why there should be a commission charge for a CFD when there is not one for a financial spread bet. The answer is that the share price embodied in a CFD is the market cash price, whereas the underlying price for a spread bet is based on the futures price, and the commission is included in the spread.

Taxation

CFDs are subject to capital gains tax in the UK under current legislation.

How do the costs of trading and profitability of a CFD compare with those of an ordinary share?

Let us take two examples for comparison.

Establishing a long position

Client A buys 4000 Lloyds TSB shares for £5 per share through his stock-broker. The charges are:

Commission	0.5%
Government stamp duty	0.5%

Client B has deposited £20,000 in his CFD account. Margin requirements for Lloyds TSB are 10 per cent. Client B purchases 20,000 Lloyds TSB CFDs at £5 each. The charges are:

Commission	0.25%
Government stamp duty	NIL

Client C places a financial spread bet to '*buy* to open' at £10 per 1p for the 'near quarter day' (70 days away). The charges are:

Commission	NIL
Government stamp duty	NIL

A dividend of 30p net is paid one month into the trade.

A financing charge is levied over two months at 2.5% above the cost of 1 month LIBOR

LIBOR is 6%.

The quotation for Lloyds TSB is '510p offered' for the near quarter day (10 weeks from now).

Clients A and B close their positions after two months at a price of £5.45.

The near future price rises to 545p bid during the eight-week period from the date that the bet was opened, and it was closed out at that price.

Opening a long position in Lloyds TSB		Client A cash purchase		Client B CFD purchase		Client C spread bet
Cash invested		£20,000 Cash deposited		£20,000 Cash deposited		£2000
Contract value	(a)	£20,000	(a)	£100,000	(a)	*£5100
Commission	(x 0.5%)	(£100)	(x 0.25%)	(£250)		NIL
Stamp duty		(£100)		NIL		NIL
Net opening costs	(c)	(£200)	(c)	(£250)	(c)	NIL
Financing costs						
Dividend	(b)	£1,200	(b)	£4,800		NIL
Interest costs		NIL		(£1,420)		NIL
Net holding costs	(d)	£1,200	(d)	£3,380		NIL
Closing the long position in Lloyds TSB						
Closing contract value	(e)	£21,800	(e)	£109,000		£5,450
Closing commission	(f)	(£109)	(f)	(£272.50)		NIL
PROFIT (a+b) – (c+d+e+f)		£2,691		£11,857.50		£350
* notional						
Return on *client's* capital employed		13.45%		59.28%		17.5%

Establishing a short position

Client A sells 8000 shares in Centrica at £2.50 through his stockbroker. The charges are:

Commission   0.5%
Government stamp duty   NIL

Client B has deposited £20,000 in his CFD account. Margin requirements for Centrica are 20 per cent. Client B sells 40,000 Centrica CFDs at £2.50 each. The charges are:

Commission   0.255%
Government stamp duty   NIL

Client C places a 'sell to open' spread bet at £10 per 1p at 247p 'bid' for the 'near quarter day' (25 days away).

An interest rebate is payable to Client B on his short position for the period that the short CFD is open at LIBID minus 2.5%.

LIBID is 5.875%.

Client B will receive an interest rebate of 3.375%.

Clients A and B close out their positions after one week at £2.40 per share. Client C closes out his position at the same time by placing 'buy to close' bet at 240p offered.

Opening a short position in Centrica		Client A cash sale		Client B CFD sale		Client C 'sell' bet to open
Equity		£20,000	deposit	£20,000	deposit	£2000
Contract value	(a)	£20,000		(a) £100,000		(a) £2470
Commission	(b)	(£100)		(b) (£250)		NIL
Stamp duty		NIL		NIL		NIL
Net opening costs		(£100)		(£250)		NIL
Interest rebate	(c)	NIL		(c) £64.73		NIL
Closing the short position in Centrica						
Closing contract value	(d)	£19,200		(d) £96,000		£2400
Closing commission	(e)	(£48)		(e) (£240)		NIL
Government stamp duty		NIL		NIL		NIL
PROFIT (a+c) – (b+d+e)		£552		£3,574.73		£70
Return on client's capital employed		2.76%		17.87%		3.5%

You can see quite clearly the advantages of trading CFDs compared with buying the shares outright, when you are considering short term trading, as compared with long term investing. Although the return on *client's* capital employed in the example for spread betting is notional, it is still a very efficient way of trading shares. You could argue that the deposit of

£2000 made by Client C represents capital employed, but such funds placed on deposit earn interest and so those earnings should be taken into consideration if a true comparison is to be made.

It is not necessary to maintain open positions for a long time when you are dealing in CFDs, because the gearing enables you to trade in considerably greater numbers of shares than a relatively small amount of capital would allow. Also, the cost of financing the purchase is a significant consideration when contemplating opening and maintaining a long position for more than a week or so. The longer you keep the long position open, the higher the price has to rise before you are likely to make worthwhile profits, or return on your capital employed. Nevertheless, the fact that a CFD has no expiry date means that you can hold the position open for longer than you may be able to do using a spread bet. Timing is the essence of making money. Thus, it may pay to use a CFD rather than a spread bet if you can get a longer period to run the position at the time that you decide to open.

> **Timing is the essence of making money**

The reasons why you cannot control the timing as to when you should open or close a position are many and various. The ways to apply analytical and technical examinations which will eliminate a great deal of the 'unknown', as well as the sources for the data needed, are described in Part Two. The alternative might be to use a Universal Stock Futures Contract.

UNIVERSAL STOCK FUTURES (USFS) COMPARED WITH CONTRACTS FOR DIFFERENCE

Universal Stock Futures, or USFs as they are called in the market, are a new derivative contract introduced by LIFFE at the end of January 2001. At first glance they appear very similar to Contracts for Difference but there are fundamental differences both in their construction as well as their costs to the investor.

A futures contract is cleared through the London Clearing House to guarantee delivery and payment. A USF is a package that is traded in the same way, but highly geared. A USF does not enjoy any different benefits or liabilities than those attaching to an ordinary future. However, it is protected in the same ways as all futures contracts. A CFD is traded outside the London Clearing House and is not entitled to the same protection.

> ⋯⋯⋯⋯A CFD is traded outside the London Clearing House ⋯⋯⋯⋯

Both contracts fall into the category of margined investment instruments which means that you do not have to put up the full contract value when you open the contract. You are only asked to lodge a percentage of the total sum due, and this is known as the margin. The amount of the margin required for a similar total contract value varies considerably between USFs and CFDs.

What your bookmaker expects from you

When you deal in CFDs, you will be asked to deposit a margin of at least £20,000 with your broker. When you deal in a USF, you will be asked to deposit £1000/£2000 with your broker.

The CFD is based on any number of shares traded in the cash market at the current price prevailing at the time that you open the contract. A USF contract is based on 1000 shares exactly based on the futures price for the selected future expiry date.

The ability to 'short' a position in shares is common to USFs, CFDs and spread betting. This practice is no longer possible in the cash market because the settlement times are so short. It is one of the major attractions for these methods of investment.

✱ EXAMPLE

Let us assume that you wish to invest approximately £10,000 in a 'short' position in Vodafone. The cash price is 243p. The September futures price is currently 241p to sell.

Capital required	USF	CFD	Spread bet
Deposit required	£10,000	£20,000	£2000

No. of shares per contract   **Cost**

CFD $\dfrac{£10,000}{243p} = 4115$ shares   say £2000 margin and finance cost @ 2% above LIBOR per annum

USF $\dfrac{£10,000}{1000 \times 241p} = 4$ Contracts*   £1400 margin

Spread bet at say £10 per 1p
price movement   NIL

*Rounded down to the nearest whole number of contracts.

Assume that one month later the cash price falls to 190p and the September futures price is 192p to buy.

Profit

CFD 4115 x 53p (243 – 190 = 53) £2180

less finance cost $\dfrac{£10,000 \times 7 \times 31}{100 \times 365} = £60 = £2120$

Return on deposit cost 10.6%

USF (243p – 192p) x 1000 x 4 = £2040   Return on deposit cost 145.7%

Spread bet 51p x £10 = £510   Return on deposit cost 25.5%

In addition to the costs shown above, there will be commissions, and any additional calls to maintain the deposit levels if the price moves against you in the intervening period between opening and closing the position. However, there should be additional income earned from interest paid on the deposit monies whilst the position is open, allocated in the same way as the financing cost.

If you invest in a CFD you may be eligible for some or all of any dividend that accrues to the underlying share. There is no right to participate in any dividend if you invest in a USF or a spread bet.

Universal Stock Futures offer investors many opportunities to enhance the performance of their equity portfolio. For example:

- they provide a quick and simple mechanism for increasing or decreasing exposure to a specific stock;

- they enable you to benefit from a predicted upward or downward movement in the value of an individual stock, whether or not you hold the share already;

- they enable capital efficient, leveraged trading as the full value of the share is not required as an up-front payment;

- they are a low cost method of investing – USFs are cash settled so they have none of the costs associated with transacting and delivering shares;

- typically, broker commissions are lower than those for share trading, starting from as low as £2 per contract;

- they allow you to switch exposure quickly from one stock to another without the costs and inconvenience of disturbing the underlying stock holding;

- they are free from the UK stamp duty which is levied on UK stocks.

All these benefits apply equally to financial spread betting.

At present, only 25 stocks are traded by LIFFE in the form of USFs. These are spread between eight countries and have been selected from the five most popular and heavily capitalized industry sectors, including telecoms, technology, banks, oils and pharmaceuticals. This list should grow throughout 2001, but only five companies in the list are resident on the London Stock Exchange, so the scope for a UK investor is pretty limited.

The authorities at LIFFE have devised this instrument as an alternative to CFDs for the ordinary investor, rather than the so-called 'expert' or professional investor. At first sight it appears to offer greater investor protection in so far as the instrument is traded through a regulated market because CFDs are traded 'off market'. However, the need to monitor the progress minute by minute whilst you have an open position running is just as strong and important whether you are using USFs, CFDs or spread bets. Don't forget that all derivatives including financial spread bets are highly geared, or leveraged, by their very nature and whilst the potential profits are a much greater percentage of capital employed, so are the potential losses. You simply cannot afford to leave any of these investments to their own devices, so to speak, while you deal with social or business commitments, without putting your hard won capital at considerable risk. You either watch it like a hawk all the time you are exposed to the market movement, or you get someone else to do it for you. Futures based trading instruments are here to stay, and you can make very substantial profits using them, provided you understand exactly how they work and you are able to control your risk sufficiently.

> all derivatives including financial spread bets are highly geared

Summary

In this chapter we have looked at Contracts for Difference (CFDs), and in particular the following aspects:

- what a CFD is, and how it is linked to margin trading, based on the cash price of a share;
- the beneficial effects of gearing with the corresponding ability to trade substantial quantities of stocks or shares for a relatively small amount of cash;
- the uses to which CFDs can be put, including hedging risk as well as short selling to make profits in a falling market;
- the right to participate in some or all of any dividends payable by the underlying company on which the CFD is based;
- the tax treatment of CFDs compared with that applicable to financial spread bets;

- comparative costs of dealing between buying a share, placing a spread bet, or investing in a CFD;

- comparisons between Universal Stock Futures, CFDs and spread betting, together with a table showing the different costs and returns on deposits.

PART TWO

Winning techniques using financial spread betting

A s we have explained in Part One there are two types of spread bet:

- intraday bets
- futures based bets.

The secret of successful financial spread betting is to reduce the 'unknown elements' to a minimum. To do this regularly, you need to have up-to-date information, and time to monitor the progress of your investments. Also, you have to understand the elements that have a direct effect on the price movement of the instrument that you have chosen. You need to know whether a change in price of another index, for example, will have a knock-on effect on your investment, and most importantly, how much time will elapse between the two events so that you can take advantage of the alteration in prices.

> The secret is to reduce the 'unknown elements' to a minimum

Intraday bets are vulnerable to movements in the futures prices of other markets, and to any major political or economic changes within market hours. The main influences are those that might possibly lead to a change in interest rates.

Futures based bets are influenced by the same considerations as intraday bets, but since their life extends over a longer period, there are several other elements that can exert pressures as well. Sector performance; results announced by competitors; markets for their products and various other factors.

The keys to successful financial spread betting are:

- *access to real time data*
- *the knowledge of how to interpret it*
- *adequate time to monitor progress and control the risk.*

Part Two of this book will guide you through the golden rules and disciplines needed to maximize your chances of winning. Remember that there is no guaranteed way to get rich, and financial spread betting carries risk. But, with sufficient real time data where necessary, as well as adequate monitoring and the proper use of guaranteed stop loss limits, you can control your potential losses and sleep well at night. If you are not too greedy you can make regular and useful profits, tax free.

6

Data required for decision making

Types of data needed to formulate decisions
Equipment needed
Sources of data
Data required

In this chapter we examine the tools that are needed for you to make your investment decisions. Your objective should be to provide yourself with the broadest possible spectrum of information, to reduce areas of risk to the minimum, without having to spend all day doing research or ploughing through masses of data, most of which is unnecessary. In particular we look at the following items:

- the type of data required
- technical analysis
- fundamental analysis
- equipment required.

TYPES OF DATA NEEDED TO FORMULATE DECISIONS

There are many different types of data that are needed for you to arrive at a decision as to whether you should open or close a trade, whether you are using spread betting or CFDs.

For the purpose of this chapter, all references to spread bets will include CFDs, and similar inclusions apply to all recommendations whether positive or negative.

There are two main types of data for short term trading:

- technical analysis
- fundamental analysis.

Technical analysis relies principally on graphs and charts for its database. Fundamental analysis is concerned with numbers, such as the report and accounts, the management, and specific information relating to the company such as products, markets, market share, competition, R&D and other factors.

> **Technical analysis relies principally on graphs and charts for its database**

Since the aim of this book is to show you ways to reduce the amount of time needed to carry out your research, I shall describe in detail the types of data that are available and then explain the vital headings that cover the areas you must investigate before making a decision.

Technical analysis

To save time, you should start with technical analysis. This is because most people find it much more convenient to see the progress of a share price graphically, rather than as a series of numbers. Consequently, if you know how to read a graph properly, you can scan through a hundred in a few minutes and pick out those few that are showing the patterns that prima facie look as if they warrant a deeper investigation. It just takes practice.

When you find a share whose price performance over the last few weeks or months looks interesting, go back as far as you can to look at the picture over the last three years at the very least.

FIG 6.1 Example of share price trend of Astrazeneca since 1995

Figure 6.1 establishes the basic trend of the share price since 1995. This trend line, when extrapolated into the future, gives you a clear value of the strongest resistance level that would be incurred if the share price continues to drop. Probably at around 2400p. That would be the level at which you would expect the market to support the share price because the attitude would be that 2400p, in this case, represents good value. However, in the meantime, the question will be 'How far is the share likely to fall in the short term?' The answer, looking at the chart, is probably to around 2800p, because there was considerable support and some resistance at that level in the past.

It is interesting to note that there has been a resistance at the 2000p level as well as at the 2400p level in the past.

Momentum is the second issue to consider. In Fig 6.1, the momentum of the price volatility in each of the years from 1995 and 1996 was minimal. It started to demonstrate considerably more movement in the second half of 1997, oscillating between a high of around 2200p in June; dropping down to a low of around 1800p (–18.18 per cent) in three months around the beginning of September; rising back to around 2100p (+16.66 per cent) in October; falling back to a low of around 1700p (–19.04 per cent) in November, and finishing the year back up again at around 2150p (+26.47 per cent).

The measurement of the time elapsed between the falls and rises is the momentum, and when each intervening period becomes shorter and shorter, the momentum is said to be rising. This is the short term trader's delight.

In Fig 6.1, the years following 1998 have confirmed the volatility, but the pattern has changed somewhat. The amounts in money terms between the highs and lows each year have increased, and the momentum of the oscillation within each annual period has remained strong, but the short term volatility has not been so marked as before, and the opportunities to make significant very short term gains in either direction have not been available.

There are many other lessons to be learned from the interpretation of chart patterns and we shall examine them later. However, it is sufficient for the purposes of this book to use Fig 6.1 to illustrate the principles of technical analysis.

Do not succumb to the temptation to regard charting as either infallible, or as being the only data you need in order to make an investment decision.

Many people get so dependent on charts or graphs that they ignore outside influences that can and do have a significant effect on the direction of movement of share prices. Pure chartists will often say 'tell me something I don't know' when you explain the historic reasons for a sudden and significant movement in a share price. What they are really saying is that historic reasons for past performances are of no interest when trying to forecast the future. Nevertheless, it is foolish to ignore what is going on in markets which can be beset by rumours, sentiment, political and economic pressures or profits and losses in other companies in the same sector, to name but a few. Thus, it is necessary to understand what fundamental analysis is, and how to use it to your advantage.

Fundamental analysis

Many books have been written about fundamental analysis, and it is not my intention to try to give a comprehensive account of the subject here. This is because fundamental analysis is particularly appropriate when considering a share for long term investment but financial spread betting is essentially very short term trading. Nevertheless, apart from analyzing the report and accounts for the last five years, as well as the Chairman's statements and getting a clear understanding of the company's products, markets, competition and reputation, there are some aspects which must be considered, and we shall describe them briefly under their general headings.

1. *Categorize each share.* Since one of the main objectives of this book is to try to enable you to learn how to improve your chances of winning, you should put all the shares that you are researching into one of three categories. These are:

    ■ *Negative.* If the general trend of the sector is negative, then that factor is likely to have a depressing effect on the price of an individual share. There is no point in trying to persuade yourself that a particular company's share is going to buck the trend, particularly over a very short period and by a sufficient margin to make a bet worth while. It is possible, but unlikely. A falling sector will produce excellent opportunities to make money out of short sellling the share by spread betting.

    ■ *Positive.* If the general trend of the sector is positive, then you stand a good chance of a short term win by spread-betting the share upwards. However, beware of the timing vis-à-vis dividend ex dates. Generally, a share price will drop by the amount of the dividend at the time that the share price goes ex-dividend on the market. It is not clever to 'buy' the share for a short term punt just before the ex-date only to see your price drop immediately after you have dealt when, with a little research, you could have got it for a cheaper price.

- *Neutral.* There will always be a number of shares that seem to miss out on positive or negative sentiment, even though they produce steady earnings, often quietly increasing earnings over several years. Such companies make ideal candidates for longer term investments rather than short term speculations. It is worth looking at the reasons why they fail to arouse interest among the investing public. As an example, the house building sector remained in the doldrums for three years from 1998, because it was thought that shares in the sector were not going to produce the mega growth compared with the technological and telecommunication company shares. The house building companies continued to produce above average yields. However, even though the 'tech' sector fell out of bed in March 2000, and base rates started to fall so that the yields on fixed interest stocks dropped, the demand for the house building companies' shares still remained depressed.

Only select shares for short term spread betting which are demonstrating strong positive or negative direction, and with strong momentum.

2. *Be aware of market sentiment.* If a share is out of favour in the market, do not try to persuade yourself that a bit of good news will change investors' perceptions. For example, if the management of a particular company has cut a dividend unexpectedly, or issued a profits warning out of the blue, the market will react like a spoilt brat and take umbrage. This resentful attitude will last for a long time, and it may even remain until the chief executive resigns, or is forced to leave.

3. *Keep abreast of press comment.* A sustained press campaign of highly critical comment can have a devastating and long lasting effect on

the share price. Marks & Spencer, Railtrack, the Channel Tunnel and Tomkins are four examples of such cases. The press threw a lot of mud at the management of these companies and quite a lot of it has stuck. Consequently, in cases such as these, you should not be lured into believing any rumours that a substantial and rapid improvement in their fortunes will happen overnight. You really do need to wait and see whether the stories are true and the market has forgiven the management before risking a bet. You will soon see if this is so by watching the share price. It does not matter if you miss the first part of the revival, there will be plenty left to go for if the sentiment really has changed for the better.

EQUIPMENT NEEDED

Hardware

All the modern desk top computers have enough capacity and speed of processing data to cope with the amount of information required to become proficient at financial spread betting.

It helps to have two VDU screens so that you can have one or two charts on display permanently, and if you use an extra screen, it allows you to see the real time price movements in sufficient detail to measure the amount of movement and establish trends, or changes in direction quickly and more accurately than if the scale of the visible graph is too small.

It is advantageous to invest in an ISDN line for your internet connection because speed in this department is essential.

It will pay you to use a service provider who allows you to have unlimited access to the internet for a fixed cost. There are several of them about, and you may find that the layout and presentation of one suits you rather better than another. Only you can decide that point.

It is much easier to make informed judgements if you have really fast data provision, as well as large VDUs to display as much of the relevant information as possible.

Software

Windows 95 or 98 or 2000 will all suffice. The best value for money and an excellent provider of the dedicated software is Trader Professional, produced by Updata Software Ltd, Updata House, Old York Road, Wandsworth, London SW18 1TG. Tel. 020 8874 4747. E-mail *sales@updata.co.uk*. Internet www.updata.co.uk.

Updata is the leading investment software company in the UK. Their Trader Professional system displays prices and news from the real time data feed transmitted via a television signal from the London Stock Exchange. This is a highly effective and cost efficient way to keep abreast of the latest developments in the financial market: The prices stream continuously through the system as they change on the exchange, and the system constantly collects and stores every price and news item so you can display price histories and search your news archive on any company. You can set alerts on key price levels or key words in news stories so that your PC almost watches the market for you.

The latest Updata package, Trader Professional II can take data from a broadcast or internet feed so you can use a system on the move, with a laptop via a GSM data card, or on your corporate network in your office. In future, you will be able to use the system on hand held devices for taking much of the hard work out of finding market opportunities.

Trader Professional gives you the tools to find accelerating stocks early, offers powerful graphical analysis and the use of 'stop losses' to lock in profits and avoid downturns. A new feature is 'Updata Community' a fully interactive, live 'chat room' enabling investors to keep in touch with each other and swap ideas and send graphs. Updata Messenger lets you see when your friends have logged in, if you are on-line.

This type of technology is designed to help investors develop a methodology to their investments, and provides the instruments and tools to make successful trading decisions.

SOURCES OF DATA

There are many sources of data but the ones described here have been chosen after trying out most of those on offer. In Chapter 7, we explain how to read the signals to enable you to control your investment decisions, and the data that we describe comes from the sources outlined below.

Newspapers and journals

The *Financial Times* is read by every person whose business includes advising other investors, or who deals in the market for brokers or fund managers. Consequently, its opinions – the Lex column in particular – exert the most influence. Opinion creates market sentiment and this is one of the most powerful factors that boosts or depresses the price of an individual share, so it is very important to know whether a share is 'in' or 'out' of favour, and the reasons why.

In addition, apart from the obvious information about the 'high' and 'low' of each share price together with its yield and PER, the table that is printed each week, showing similar data about the separate sectors, provides invaluable information, enabling you to establish the background to each share for comparative purposes.

The 'City comment' sections of *The Times*, the *Sunday Times*, the *Daily Telegraph*, the *Sunday Telegraph*, the *Daily Mail*, the *Mail on Sunday*, the *Glasgow Herald* and the *Scotsman* are all worth reading.

The *Investors Chronicle* is a good reference work and you should use it to get a potted view of the business of any company in which you may become interested, together with an opinion of its management and products. It is published once a week on Fridays.

Internet services

You will need to have the up-to-date spread bet quotations of a financial bookmaker on your screen whilst you have an intraday bet running. The website of Cantorindex is very clearly set out, and the prices are revised every 30 seconds. It has one huge advantage over the other bookmakers' real time quote screens – namely, it is free. You do not even have to have an account open with Cantorindex to see their prices, as you do with the other firms.

For corporate news stories and a wealth of data you will need to have access to FT MarketWatch and Bloomberg.com.UK and these two programs are also free. Between these two, you will be able to get enough historic as well as breaking news to occupy your day completely, should you so wish. At first, you will probably feel overwhelmed by the sheer volume of information that is available, and you will feel that unless you read it all, you will miss some vital piece of news. Don't worry. A lot of it will be repeated, and it only requires a bit of practice to be able to skim through the mass of copy to pick out the details of the few shares where you have got open spread bets in your current portfolio.

You start with the name of the share that you have got from scrolling through the charts first, and you use the text comment to build up a case either for or against placing a bet. Do not do it the other way round.

DATA REQUIRED

The following data is required in the first case to decide whether to place a bet at all, and subsequently to monitor the progress of the bet and control the risk.

Intraday bets

You will need access to all financial news items affecting the particular index you have selected.

- If you choose the FTSE 100 index you will require all the news items from 0600 hours until 0930 hours and from then onwards, until you close out the bet.

- If you select the Dow Jones Industrial Average you will require any major world economic indicator news from 0600 hours until 1430 hours, such as changes in interest rates by any European or Far Eastern central bank; changes in crude oil or gas prices; outbreaks of military conflicts; major earthquakes in cities, or any major financial failures such as banks or large companies with global presence or worldwide markets.

■ A constant monitoring and record of the following indices from 0745 hours onwards, until you decide either to omit a bet for the day, or to close out a bet:
- the daily FTSE cash
- the near quarter day FTSE Future
- the daily DAX 30 Future
- the near quarter day DAX 30 Future
- the daily CAC 40 Future
- the next month CAC 40 Future
- the daily Wall Street cash (Dow Jones)
- the near quarter day Wall Street Future (Dow Jones)
- the daily S&P Future
- the near quarter day S&P 500 Future
- the daily Nasdaq Future
- the near quarter day Nasdaq Future.

■ Either a full screen chart showing one of the two indices, or a minimum of a half-screen chart showing the progress of the FTSE 100 or the Dow Jones, in either case with real time price updates. If there is *any* delay in price updating, you will be wasting your time and money.

■ The current quotations of at least one financial spread bookmaker, preferably two. They should be updated at least every 30 seconds throughout market hours.

At first sight this list may seem daunting. It really is very simple when you get used to looking at the data, and when you understand how to use it. It is no different from learning how to drive a car. Can you remember your first reactions when you were faced with all the instruments on the dashboard and you were told that you had to watch them as well as to keep your eyes on the road to avoid hitting someone or something?

The reason for needing to monitor all this data is that you will then be able to calculate the risk/reward chances, or odds, on winning. You will realize that since the different indices are moving all the time, and because they exert influences on each other, the chances, or odds either against you winning or in your favour are moving all the time. If you want to maximize your chances of winning, you need to understand how they are calculated and how and why they are constantly changing. If you can remain in control of a situation that is always fluid, you will stand a far better chance of making money compared with the uninitiated person who simply goes by a 'hunch'. We shall explain how and why these influences operate in Chapter 7, and how you calculate the odds which are varying all the time.

> **It is simple when you get used to the data**

The need to understand these elements is so important for intraday betting because of the volatility that is inherent in betting on an index. The FTSE 100 and the Dow Jones can move 20 or 30 points *up and down* in a day, and frequently do so and the Dow Jones is even more volatile than the FTSE 100. The Nasdaq often moves 50 or 60 points in both directions, which is one of the reasons why it is not recommended in this book, except for the very brave! The other reason is because the momentum in the Nasdaq can be so great that you can be wiped out in a few seconds, and it does not seem to be sensible to become exposed to such unnecessary risk voluntarily.

Futures based bets

The data required for futures based bets is somewhat different. There is more time to get your bet right, or wait to see if it will recover, if it goes against you by a small amount initially. Consequently, you will want to look at several other categories of data.

Prices

As explained earlier, bookmakers' quotations are based upon the futures price of a share, or index, rather than the cash price. Remember also that whilst there is a correlation between the two, they do not necessarily move in tandem, at the same time, or by the same amount. Nevertheless, since the most accessible price is usually the cash, you can start by monitoring that one first, and look at the futures if there is a significant move in the cash price.

Summary

In this chapter we have examined the tools that you need to provide the data required to make value judgements as to whether or not to make bets, and the equipment, both hardware and software, which will save you time finding suitable candidates to back. We have looked at the following items:

- data required, including access to real time prices;
- technical analysis of the most up-to-date price movements for intraday bets;
- fundamental analysis and sources of data for futures based bets;
- hardware including an ISDN telephone line and adequate computer equipment with two VDUs;
- software that will give you real time prices for all the major indices as well as share prices for the FTSE 100, 250 and 350 and real time chart updates for all the shares and news feed.

7

Reading the signals

In this chapter we look at the signals that are available and how to read them. In particular we describe:

- the different chart signals;
- how to recognize those that are positive and those that are negative;
- disciplines required;
- the vital need to monitor open bets continuously;
- placing *buy* and *sell* bets at the same time;
- arbitraging;
- risk assessment.

We shall start by explaining how charts are built up. I make no apologies, if that seems very basic, because it is only too easy to forget how the building blocks are created for any analytical device that one uses frequently. It is only by a complete understanding of what the tools are that you will be able to make them work efficiently for you. It is these basic pictorial representations of data, unfolding before your eyes in real time that will give you the control of your investment risk, as well as enabling you to anticipate future wins or losses in the value of each bet.

THE SIGNALS

Steps

The first thing to understand is that generally, price movements tend to go in steps, rather than straight lines. The overall pattern will consist of small movements which, when viewed over a short time period, look something like the pattern shown in Fig 7.1.

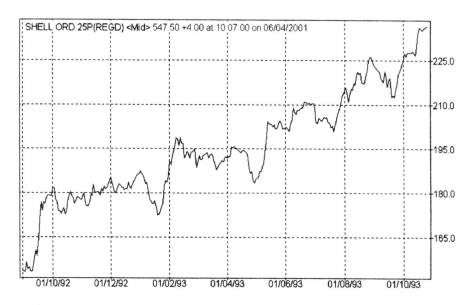

FIG 7.1 An example of price movements in steps

I have chosen a share price chart which covers a period of 12 months, but Fig 7.1 illustrates exactly the point that I am making. This pattern could easily have been spread over one trading day, and that is normally what you will find. Instead of a number of weeks being shown along the horizontal axis, it would normally be hours during the day that appear. Every time there is a movement in the share price it will be shown as a new position on the chart and the lines simply connect and record the changing values. Two facts can be deduced immediately from Fig 7.1.

First, the *trend* of the price was upwards, and it was sustained, albeit in this case over rather a long time.

Second, the business transacted in this share over the period was sustained. Certainly there were more buyers for the shares than there were sellers. Demand outstripped supply. Had the demand dropped off, and sellers outnumbered buyers, the price would have dropped and the trend changed direction. Such a variable pattern can be found in the plot of a price movement during a day, reflecting the market sentiment towards an individual share. The market sentiment is reflecting the majority of buyers over sellers, or vice versa from hour to hour. These facts are incontrovertible, and without going any further to find out anything more about the company, the chart indicates that the rise in share price should be sustained.

Very often, of course, the pattern will change direction over a short period, whether it be one day or in the course of a week or a month. An upward trend will change to a downward one, and vice versa. There are several well known and highly regarded short term patterns that will indicate an impending change of direction, such as 'head and shoulders' and 'double bottom' and others which I shall be describing later on with explanations how to use them to your advantage, but at this stage the discussion will be confined to describing what the patterns are, so that, with practice, you will recognize them quickly. Generally the share price record will move in steps. You must establish the trend.

Trend

The trend will show you at a glance whether the share price is rising or falling over a given period. It is one of the main attractions for using spread betting that you can make money from a share price that is falling, just as easily as you can from one that is rising. What you have to do is to

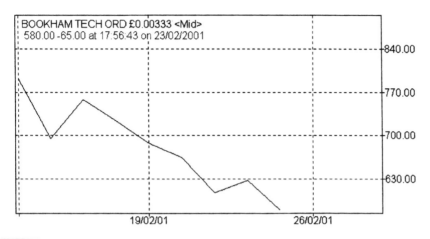

FIG 7.2 Angle of trend favouring a sell bet

find one that has established either an upward or downward trend and then use it to your advantage. It is just like looking for an up or a down escalator, and the best ones are those where the trend is established at an angle of about 45 degrees.

Figure 7.2 is a perfect example of a trend following just the right sort of angle for a trader to back with a *sell* bet. If the trend were to be pointing upwards instead of downwards, it would give a strong signal to place a *buy* bet.

It is attractive for another reason also. The momentum is sufficiently strong for you to expect to see a continuation of the trend over a short time, in this case it is showing a falling price. It has fallen from around 775p on 12 February to 580p on 23 February, or 195p over 11 days. A *sell* bet at £10 per 1p would bring a handsome profit if it were to fall another 100p, and on the historic data available to you that position should be achieved over the next six days.

Exactly the same disciplines apply to a share price with a rising trend.

Figure 7.3 is a good example of a share with an established rising price trend and it embodies good momentum with an angle of climb that makes it a prime candidate for a *buy* bet. This example was taken from the bigger picture shown in Fig 7.4, and that also has some very important lessons which can be seen easily.

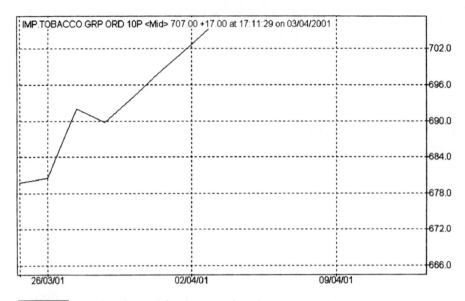

FIG 7.3 Angle of trend favouring a buy bet

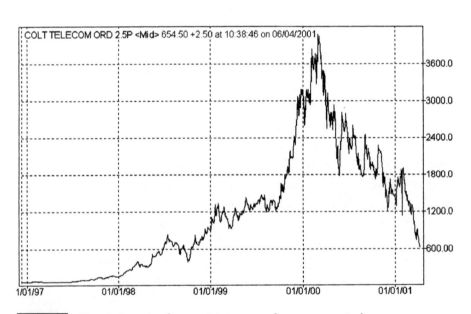

FIG 7.4 Momentum in share prices over a four-year period

Momentum

Momentum is a very important ingredient needed in a share price pattern for successful spread betting. Think of the amount of 'energy' that is being exhibited by the share price which shows up as oscillations on the chart, rather like the print-out of the violence of terrestrial movement during an earthquake. In the case of a share price, the momentum may be coupled with a strong trend, whether it is rising or falling. Occasionally you will find one where the trend is horizontal, but you should avoid it because there will not be any strong signal as to which direction the trend will take, and you could be caught out badly.

For three years, from 1997 until 2000, there was very little momentum in the share price showing in Fig 7.4. The trend was upward and this climb accelerated from around August 1999 until about March when the fall in price was equally rapid until about May. At this point, the share price bounced off the 1800p level three times over the space of four or five months, each 'bounce' representing a good betting opportunity, both upwards and downwards, over a short period. The momentum creating frequent opportunities to win, compared with the more pedestrian performance over the earlier years shown on the chart.

Trading ranges

As we have demonstrated, share prices generally move in steps, whether up or down, from one plateau to another and consolidate for a period. So having first established the trend, i.e. direction, the next step is to establish the trading range.

Figure 7.5 shows how to plot the trading range of a share, whether it be over a period of 12 months, as shown in the figure, or over a shorter or longer period. It is a very simple operation, and the only rules are that you link the 'highs' and the 'lows' by drawing lines on the chart, and the lines *must be parallel*. This superimposition of parallel lines defines the trading range of a share price and it makes it very easy for you to predict where the share price is going to go next, *and to calculate the amount by which the price will change.* You can do this quite simply by reference to the vertical axis which is measured in pence.

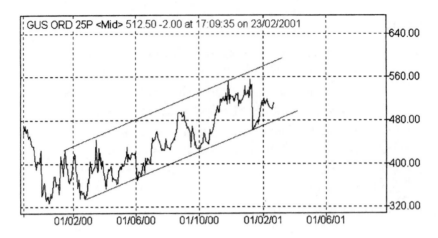

GUS ORD 25P <Mid> 512.50 -2.00 at 17:09:35 on 23/02/2001

640.00	
560.00	
480.00	
400.00	
320.00	

01/02/00   01/06/00   01/10/00   01/02/01   01/06/01

FIG 7.5 Trading range over a 12 month period

The distance between the 'highs', and the distance between the 'lows', can be measured on the horizontal axis which is measured in time, whether it be hours or minutes as you would see when analyzing an intraday chart, or days, weeks or months, if you are analyzing an individual share price chart to decide whether to make a futures based bet.

Lesson. First establish whether the trend is up, down or horizontal. Then superimpose parallel lines to see whether there is sufficient 'room' between the highs and lows to warrant a bet, and whether the time taken to oscillate between the highs and lows gives you enough time for the price to move sufficiently to produce a win before the futures date expires. We shall be examining this aspect in more detail in Chapter 8.

Chart breakout

Figures 7.6 and 7.7 provide good examples of chart breakout.

Not only has the share price broken out from its previously established trading range, but it has formed a new one at a higher level.

Whatever the direction of the trend may be, at some stage the price will break out from between the parallel lines imposed by establishing the trading range. This breakout direction can be upwards or down-

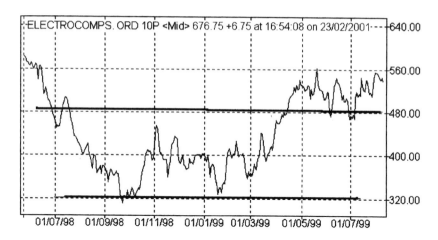

FIG 7.6 Breakout with new trading range at higher level

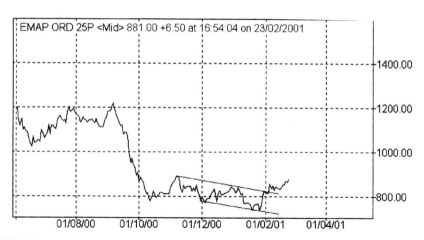

FIG 7.7 Breakout after downward trend

wards, and it is dangerous to risk a bet on the share price following the new direction before it has established a new pattern and settled into it.

Forecasting 'highs' and 'lows'

The whole purpose of financial spread betting is to make profits by forecasting accurately whether an individual share price will rise or fall *far enough* to produce a net profit after allowing for the spread in the price. The question is, will the movement in the share price run out of steam before the minimum amount of movement needed to break even?

The best way to describe how to establish the limits is to imagine that the share price is a bouncing ball. Draw horizontal lines across the chart linking both the high points as well as the low points. You have to be fairly arbitrary as to the starting points, but the only important aspect is that they must be horizontal.

FIG 7.8   Example of support and resistance levels

Now imagine that the lines represent floor levels in a block of flats, and that the share price is a bouncing ball. When it hits the floor of one level, it will bounce up and down between the floor and the ceiling of the flat above. Whilst it is oscillating between those two levels, the 'floor' of that flat is known as a support level, and the 'ceiling' is known as a resistance level.

If the share price (ball) goes through the ceiling upwards to the next level, that is a chart breakout. The level that previously was the ceiling becomes the next floor, or support level, and the next ceiling above becomes the new resistance level.

If the share price breaks out downwards, then the previous floor, or support level becomes the new ceiling, or resistance level and the new floor becomes the new support level.

These levels, although somewhat arbitrary and difficult to predict precisely, will serve as your benchmarks for measuring the point at which the share price is likely to run out of energy on the way up, and the points at which the share price is likely to stop falling on the way down.

Figure 7.9 is a fine example of historic data being a good pointer to the minimum potential profit that you could make under the circumstances depicted.

FIG 7.9   **Historic data indicating minimal potential profit**

In Fig 7.9, the trend overall has been upward since early in 1998, and it ran upwards for all that year. During 1999 the overall trend was lateral until it fell out of bed during the last couple of months, and continued on downwards for the first two months of 2000. Since then, it has climbed back up at a very similar angle to that of its fall until the Autumn of that year, when the trend line changed to a much more acceptable angle of about 45 degrees. The first lesson from the data in Fig 7.9 is that *the trend over the near future should continue upwards at the same level.*

How far upwards is the price likely to rise before the impetus stops? Figure 7.9 shows very clearly the price levels reached by the previous 'highs'. In fact it is easy to see that the price will probably struggle to rise much above 770p. But it should get to 750p at least, and so there is a very good chance of winning about 40 x your stake without being either greedy, or unreasonable in your expectations. This level is certainly achievable and realistic. The second lesson arising from Fig 7.9 is that *you should use historic 'highs' to set your next target price level, provided that they were achieved recently.*

Flags

We have explained that prices move up or down in a series of steps, and you will see from Fig 7.10 that they very often move sideways after a rise or fall into a pattern that is called a flag. They look like two sides of a triangle converging towards a point, and they are very easy to recognize.

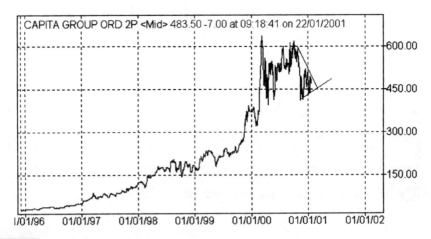

FIG 7.10 Example of a flag

There are several points to remember when you see a flag, because they will give you a very strong clue as to which direction the price is going to move next.

Lesson 1 The shape of the 'triangle' is formed because the oscillation of the share price gets less and less over the time period. The consecutive levels of the highs get lower, and the consecutive levels of the lows get higher. *When the flag looks as if it is getting to a point, the share price will break out violently, either upwards or downwards.*

Do not bet on the future direction of the share price when you see a flag forming.

Lesson 2 It is possible to see the formation of a flag pattern over a long time. Perhaps one leg of the triangle started to form as far back as a year or more. The basic principles applying to an unpredictable price break-out still apply, although you may well be able to place several winning bets during the build up of the flag pattern. Figure 7.11 illustrates this point well.

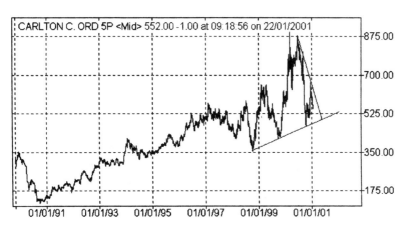

FIG 7.11 Example of the slow formation of a flag pattern

Triangle alignment

Sometimes the shape of the flag consists of one of the lines forming part of the triangle being horizontal and the other being at an angle.

Figure 7.12 demonstrates several points. First, as I have explained earlier, when the 'energy' embodied in the oscillations gets compressed to a point, the price breakout is often violent. Second, after the share price has broken out, it will establish itself by consolidating at a new level, and

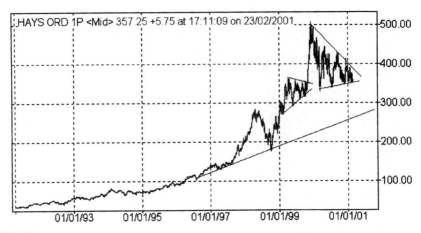

HAYS ORD 1P <Mid> 357.25 +5.75 at 17:11:09 on 23/02/2001

FIG 7.12 Flags showing lines at angles and horizontal lines

then move sideways for a time. It is creating a new step, whether the direction be up or down. Third, the *angle* of one of the legs is horizontal and the other is lying at about 45 degrees.

Lesson 3 More often than not, the price level demonstrated by the *horizontal* leg represents either a support level, or a resistance level, depending upon which leg it is.

If, as is shown in Fig 7.12, the horizontal leg is the lower one and the price keeps bouncing off that price, whilst the upper leg is demonstrating a rapid succession of lower 'highs', then any break out downward is likely to be violent, whereas any breakout upwards is likely to be muted. This is because the horizontal leg, in such circumstances, is forming a support level.

The opposite result will be likely to occur with a breakout in the opposite direction if the horizontal leg is forming a resistance level. Any upward movement would be stronger than any downward movement.

Significant patterns

There are several patterns that can occur in the build up of a chart of an individual share price, or during the day for an index. They are strong signals which you ignore at your peril. They can be very useful friends and I strongly advise you to be alert to them, whenever you see them forming, and to be prepared to accept their warning.

Double bottoms

Whenever you see a double bottom, or even a triple bottom, formed on a chart, the signal means that the next movement of the share price will be *upwards*.

Figure 7.13 is a classic example of a triple bottom which occurred during the month of July 2000, in the share price chart of Abbey National.

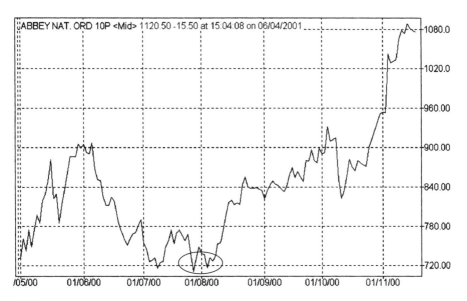

FIG 7.13 Example of a triple bottom

Figure 7.13 also displays a good example of a classic 'cup' shape over the period between the beginning of June and the first ten days of August. At that time, the share price had reached 780p, which, coupled with the triple bottom just prior to that date, meant that you would have been safe to bet that the price would continue to rise.

How high might it go before running out of steam? As I have said earlier, look at the recent historic data and you can see that the most recent 'high' peaked at around 900p. However, you would have been alert to the fact that there had just been a resistance level at around 780p, so you would have been sensible to have waited to see if the price achieved a break out sufficiently above that level to establish the fact that it was a genuine change of trading range, and you could have placed a *buy* bet at around 800p, with a target of 900p.

Figure 7.14 illustrates the opposite formation to the classic cup shape shown in Fig 7.13. If you start from around the second week in July 1999, when the share price started to climb from about 152p, and you imagine that you are at around 1 February 2000, you might have been tempted to place a *buy* bet when the price kicked upwards a bit. The trend was downwards. The trading range had not been penetrated. The dome shape was still intact. All the signs are for a continued fall in the price. You would have had better odds in your favour to place a *sell* bet.

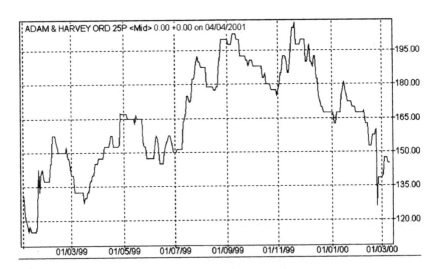

FIG 7.14 **Example of figures showing a dome shape**

Double top

The pattern known as a double top is the precursor to a share price falling.

There are several instances of double tops in Fig 7.15. They occurred, for instance, during the two years 1990–92, and in a more pronounced fashion during the two years 1992–94, and very clearly during 1998 when the price fell substantially after a very steep rise.

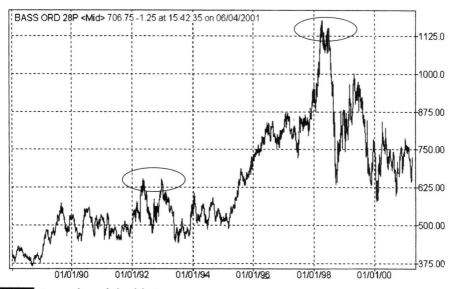

BASS ORD 28P <Mid> 706.75 -1.25 at 15:42:35 on 06/04/2001

FIG 7.15 Examples of double tops

If you see a double top forming, it is a strong invitation to place a *sell* bet, and you will be unlikely to lose.

Head and shoulders

This pattern can be seen several times in Fig 7.16. The most obvious occurrence took place in 1998, but there were others showing in 1999 and 2000.

Very often you will see the pattern forming on a larger scale chart, which does not show up quite so clearly when you look over a much longer period.

This point is clearly illustrated in Fig 7.17, which depicts the movement of the FTSE 100 during a period of 30 minutes on 5 April 2001.

A head and shoulders formation indicates that the share price will fall after the right hand 'shoulder' appears. It is not such a strong signal as are double bottoms or double tops, but the share price will definitely fall. One of the problems is that you cannot really forecast just how far the price will drop, but there tends to be a certain symmetry to the pattern generally, and so you would probably expect it to go back down to around its previous level before it started to create the pattern.

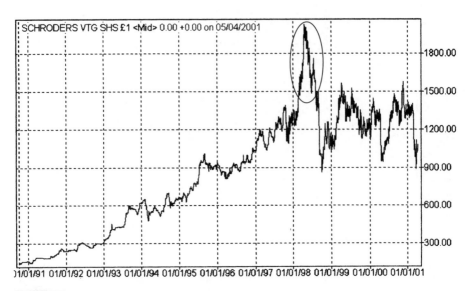

FIG 7.16 Example of head and shoulders

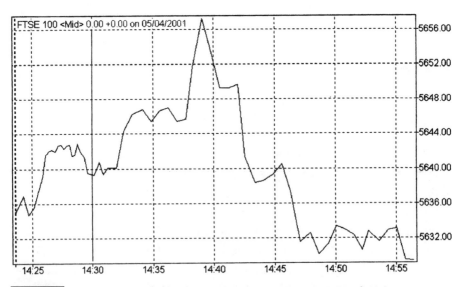

FIG 7.17 Movements of the FTSE over 30 minutes on 5 April 2001

In Fig 7.17, you can see that the trend line changed direction from that which it had adopted between 1440 and 1447, when it broke out upwards from the trading range. For the next seven minutes it created a new trading range, and then broke out downwards.

Reverse head and shoulders

This pattern is clearly shown in Fig 7.18, and it occurred in 1996, 1997 and 1998. Any constraints on the extent of the recovery will be imposed by looking at the historic patterns of highs and lows, to give you an indication as to where you might expect the price to stop moving.

FIG 7.18 Reverse head and shoulders

▌POSITIVE AND NEGATIVE RECOGNITION

It will help you to comply with the disciplines needed to minimize your downside risk, as well as to arrive at realistic and achievable targets for profit if you familiarize yourself with the different positive and negative signals. It will become second nature to you with practice, and these are the first steps towards adopting a professional approach to your risk control.

However, there is one important point to remember. We are concerned with financial spread betting, not investing in the conventional sense. All the teaching and received wisdom rammed down the throats of every investor concentrates on finding ways to make profits when markets are rising. When they go into reverse, all the financial tipsters and market commentators look for shares to buy that are likely to buck the downward trend, and increase in price. But *not* spread betters. We can make profits just as easily, and very often more quickly, in a falling market as we can in a rising one. Consequently, the question of positive or negative signals and the need to recognize and act on them depends upon which way you are betting.

Betting on a rise in price

Positive signs are:

- double bottom
- triple bottom
- cup shape
- reverse head and shoulders
- chart breakout upwards.

Negative signs are:

- double top
- triple top
- dome shape
- head and shoulders
- chart breakout downwards.

Betting on a falling price

Positive signs are:

- double top

- triple top
- dome shape
- head and shoulders
- chart breakout downwards.

Negative signs are:

- double bottom
- triple bottom
- cup shape
- reverse head and shoulders
- chart breakout upwards.

DISCIPLINES REQUIRED

The one significant difference between the amateur and the professional over the whole spectrum of investment can be summed up in a simple phrase – 'the willingness to cut a loss quickly'. The amateur will always hang on too long whilst watching the loss grow visibly, whereas the professional will cut the position quickly when it is obvious that things have started to go wrong.

> The amateur will always hang on too long

The old adage in the City that says 'the first cut is the cheapest cut' is as true today as it was before the violent volatility in share prices came to stay.

One of the staple ingredients of financial spread betting is the substantial amount of gearing that is built into the structure. It is one of the main reasons for using the system for investment. But it can be as damaging to your wealth if it starts acting against you, as it is beneficial to your bank balance when it is working in your favour.

Don't be afraid to close a bet soon after you have opened it, if the price turns against you.

It amazes me how many people will sit watching a price moving against them and do nothing. It is almost as if they are mesmerised and petrified, like a rabbit when it knows that a stoat has singled it out for dinner. The natural characteristic of the average British investor is not to do anything in haste. There is a view, widely held, that if a share price falls after it has been bought, it should be left alone to recover in due course and that, consequently, there can be no question of selling it at a loss because by holding on, it will probably recover and show a profit. How much this attitude is due to wishful thinking, and how much it may be attributed to an unwillingness to admit to bad judgement at the time the share was bought is unclear. You have only to look at the charts to see what sort of horrendous losses you can take if you hang on too long when the market sentiment turns against your particular investment.

You are the only one in control of your exposure to risk, and you have only got yourself to blame if you take no action when all the warning signs are there to see clearly.

There is no reason to feel guilty when cutting a loss. It is the mark of a professional and you should feel satisfied that your quick action has preserved as much of your wealth as possible, rather than let it be eroded further.

MONITOR YOUR BETS CLOSELY

Remember that all the time that you have a bet open, your capital is at risk. The more volatile the price of the subject of your bet, the greater the risk. The speed of price change can be very fast indeed.

No one can get their forecasts right all the time, and there are often events that occur that are impossible to foresee which can turn a trend on its head in a trice. Over and over again I have stressed the fact that volatility is here to stay. Also, the spread better *needs* volatility to create winning opportunities, and volatility brings dangers as well as winning chances.

Events can take dramatic turns against you, as well as helping you considerably. We shall discuss this aspect in more detail in Chapter 8 when we examine ways to win. One of the secrets of success is the need to monitor your bets closely. This is particularly true if you are using intraday betting on indices as your chosen investment medium.

The imposition of stop loss limits will help to prevent a potential loss from becoming catastrophic, but you will suffer from consequent widening of the spreads, and thereby reduce your potential profits. In the final analysis, the responsibility for managing your risk is yours alone, and the only way to exercise control is by monitoring the performance and progress of your bet *constantly* while the bet is running.

PLACING BUY AND SELL BETS AT THE SAME TIME

I am often asked whether it makes sense to place a buy and a sell bet at the same time on the FTSE 100 or Dow Jones or Nasdaq Indices, in view of their volatility. There are two points to consider if you think of betting in this way.

First, no financial bookmaker will accept such bets, whether it be for an index or an individual share. Consequently, if you want to pursue this course of action, you will have to open several accounts with other bookmakers, and this can lead to administrative hazards. It is perfectly possible to do this, but with some further research you may find that the game is not really worth the candle.

> there is a substantial degree of risk in this operation

Second, there is a substantial degree of risk built into this operation, and the best way to illustrate it is to use an example of what might happen.

Figure 7.19 shows the FTSE 100 Index.

Suppose that you had placed a buy and a sell bet at 5805 at around 0930. For the purpose of this illustration I am ignoring the spread. Unless you closed out the buy at around 5830 (and in this example there were two opportunities so to do which is most unusual), and assuming that you left both bets to run until the close of business when the index closed at 5795, your profit would be 10 points *minus two* amounts of spread. You

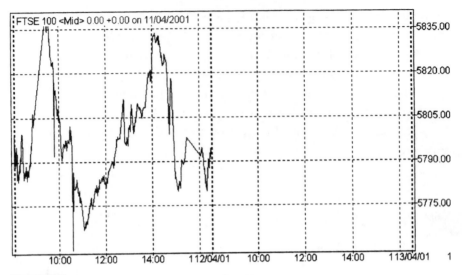

FIG 7.19 **FIG 7.19** FTSE 100 Index on 11 April 2001

would almost certainly end up showing a net loss. Not clever. Alternatively, suppose that you opened your betting by placing a buy bet at 5805, and subsequently placed a sell bet at 5825 without closing out the original buy bet, when the index was on the way down. All you would have achieved would be a profit of 20 points, before allowing for two sets of spreads. Any subsequent rise or fall in the index will be counterbalanced by the 'sell' or 'buy' bets that are running in the opposite direction.

ARBITRAGING

The practice known as arbitrage depends upon your ability to buy and sell, or to sell and buy *simultaneously* either in different markets, or in the same markets using different bookmakers. For example, suppose you saw the following situation:

Current date	Index/share	Futures date	Price quoted	
			Bookmaker A	Bookmaker B
9 April 2001	FTSE 100	19 June 2001	6560 – 6566	6553 – 6559

If you buy at 6559 from Bookmaker B, for say £1000 per point, and *simultaneously* sell at 6560 to Bookmaker A, for the same stake, you would make a profit of £1000 instantly.

I want to stress the dangers of playing this game. With the degree of volatility in the index markets, and the speed of change in the prices quoted, you run a very real risk of being unable to close out the bet at the price you need and this results in a strong chance of making a substantial loss.

RISK ASSESSMENT

The ability to assess the degree of risk over the future performance of the index or the individual share price moving up or down is the key to success in financial spread betting. So the question is – 'How do we do it?' The answer, in very simple terms, lies in three basic sources of data, two of which you will get from charts.

First. *Is the share oversold or overbought?*

This is a very easy question to answer, and there are two sources of data.

- The *Financial Times*. At the back of the FT there is a table shown every day called the 'FTSE Actuaries Share Indices'. A subdivision of this table is entitled 'FT Actuaries Industry Sectors'. This table is divided into headings which link to the categories inside the paper where the individual share price/earnings (PER) data is displayed. The table shows the average yield, dividend cover and PER for the sector or category, and you can easily compare the data for an individual share with that of the sector or category. If the PER is below the sector or category average, the price will probably turn upwards, and if the PER is above the average, the price will probably turn down.

- *The chart for an individual share price over at least two years, preferably five years.* From this data you can see immediately whether the share price trend is up or down, or horizontal. You can establish the values of recent highs, lows, resistance and support levels, as well as the degree of momentum. Also, depending upon whether the share appears to be oversold or overbought after comparison of its PER with that of the category, you can see from the chart whether the trend is increasing the gap away from the average, or whether it is bringing the PER closer to the average figure.

Second. *Where is the share price within the current established trading range?* You can see the answer to this question at a glance by looking at the chart. With regular practice you will be able to spot both opportunities as well as warning signs very quickly.

■ Remember, the trading range must have been established for long enough for you to be able to make a short term forecast with confidence.

Third. *What is the market sentiment?* The answer to this question is written large over all the City pages of the newspapers and financial journals. You will be more likely to win if you follow these basic precepts.

■ *Don't try and buck the trend.* If a category or sector is out of favour, do not be persuaded by some glib tipster to place a buy bet on a share whose price has been falling like a stone. When such conditions prevail, it is only too easy to persuade yourself that a particular share looks cheap. It probably does when compared to its recent 'high', but since it has been falling out of bed, today's price may well seem expensive tomorrow.

■ *Wait until the price has turned within the trading range.* If you don't wait until the price has turned within the trading range parameters, you risk being caught by a chart break out. Also, the fact that the share price has followed the pattern of behaviour established by the trading range limits confirms that the market sentiment has remained unchanged.

■ *When market sentiment changes for one share, check your open bets for risk/reward.* If market sentiment changes as a result of lower than expected results for one share, or a profit warning, for example, immediately close out any bet in a share in the same category if the news is bad. Alternatively, increase your stake if the news is good.

- *Be alert to changes to the economic indicators.* Any major alteration to the economic indicators will have an effect on some or all share prices, depending upon how vulnerable the category or sector is to that particular factor. Interest rate changes will affect all financials, and any company with large amounts of debt. Oil price rises will affect all transport costs. Reduction in the price of crude oil below US$15 per barrel makes it uneconomic for the exploration companies to operate. Increased unemployment means that companies with large numbers of employees will be able to keep down the cost of labour. Reductions in the Retail Price Index (RPI) will reduce the amount of demands for increases in wage awards.

> Be alert to changes to the economic indicators

Summary

In this chapter we have examined the following tools which you need to master if you are to reduce exposure to risk to a minimum:

- the chart signals that will tell you when to place a 'buy' or a 'sell' bet;
- the ways to estimate the amount of the potential winning, or profits;
- the signals which alert you to a change in the anticipated direction of a share price;
- the disciplines that are needed to preserve your capital;
- the essential need to monitor any open positions while a bet is running;
- the attractions and dangers of arbitraging; and
- what factors you need to know in order to assess the risks attached to betting on any individual share.

8

Golden rules for successful financial spread betting

Intraday bets on an index
Futures based bets on an individual share
How to calculate the odds
Risk warning

In this chapter we bring together the advice and information described in the rest of the book to give you the golden rules for successful financial spread betting. We include a list of dos and don'ts which has been built up from experience, and they should become an ingrained part of your approach to this form of investment. You should run through the checklist automatically every time you are considering placing a bet, rather like the pre-flight routine that airline pilots carry out before they switch on the engines.

In particular we discuss the following factors that you should consider, depending on the type of financial spread bet that you are contemplating, together with the dos and don'ts to increase your chances of successful bets.

- intraday bets on an index
- futures based bets on an individual share
- how to calculate the odds.

The gearing, or leverage, on all financial spread bets and contracts for difference is very great. Never forget that although this aspect can work substantially to your advantage when you get it right, the converse is also true and your losses can mount up very fast indeed if the market moves against you. Monitor your bets at all times while they are open and running.

INTRADAY BETS ON AN INDEX

As we have shown, intraday bets are very short term investments. You are looking for an instrument where the price movement is following a pattern that is as configured in such a way that the chances are that you can predict the direction of the next movement and, to some extent, the amount by which it will rise, fall or go horizontally, with some degree of certainty. In other words, the odds on your prediction being right are greater than those that it may be wrong, over a very short period. It could be minutes, it could be an hour or two.

> intraday bets are very short term investments

The volatility of indices, such as the FTSE 100, the Dow Jones Industrial Average, Standard and Poor 500, Nasdaq, Hang Seng, Dax and Cac, and others is massive, and here to stay. It is quite common for the first five listed above to fluctuate a combined amount of 80 points (up 40 from the start and back to the start and down another 40 points in one trading session. The first hour of trading on the London market, and the first half hour of trading on the US markets, are not representative of the true market trend. During those periods, limit orders are being registered on the screens, and the market makers are not obliged to put up their prices until 0900 in London.

- *Never risk more money than you can afford to lose*
- *Wait to see where the market is heading before you commit yourself to opening a bet*

When you want to bet on the FTSE 100 Index, you must always be aware of the prices being made by the futures markets as well as those being quoted by the financial bookmakers on the following indices, from 0800 every market day until the close of business:

- Dow Jones Industrial Average
- S&P 500
- Nasdaq
- Techmark
- CAC
- Dax.

If they are all in positive territory, i.e. showing upward trends, you can expect London to follow suit, *unless* there are any economic announcements due that day which might depress the market. You cannot legislate for unexpected announcements concerning earnings forecasts from individual companies such as BP Amoco, Vodafone, Shell, BT, Glaxo Wellcome or SmithKline Beecham, or any of the heavily weighted shares. I have seen a profits warning from Vodafone alone reverse an established upward trend in the FTSE 100 Index and turn a profitable bet into a loss in the space of a few seconds.

The index which exerts the strongest influence over the FTSE 100 is the S&P 500. The CAC and the Dax are lightweight by comparison, and you can ignore them unless both are showing a *strong* direction opposite to that being exhibited by the FTSE 100. The Nasdaq is very volatile and will often be trending in the opposite direction to the S&P 500. When that happens, it is a question of which one exerts enough influence in the US market to win the tug-of-war. However they will influence some movement in the FTSE 100, and since they will be fighting it out after our market has closed, you are best advised to leave the bet alone under those circumstances.

The domestic economic announcements that can have a dramatic effect on the direction of the FTSE 100 Index are announced in the UK at 0930. These will include statistics on unemployment, retail prices index, purchasing managers index, consumer price index, and others. Announcements concerning interest rates – whether changes or otherwise – are usually made at midday.

You should wait to see what the announcements are before opening a bet on the days when they are due.

Announcements in the US concerning non-farm payrolls (unemployment figures) and the other indices described above are usually made at 1430 London time. Changes in the Federal Reserve Discount Rate (interest rates) are usually made at around 1530 London time, or later, after our market has closed. These announcements can often have a substantial effect on our market.

Be aware of what announcements are due from the US during any given day, and beware of the possible consequences in London. The monthly review of the Federal Reserve Discount Rate will always hold back trade in London until after it has been announced, as will any advertised comment or economic review due to be made by the chairman of the Federal Reserve Bank. When such events are going to take place, it adds to the risks involved in forecasting the likely direction that an index will take.

The main difference between an amateur and a professional spread better, or punter at a horse or dog race meeting, is this – the amateur *always* bets too often.

> the amateur **always** bets too often

- *Make sure that you have checked* **all** *the potential risks* **and** *calculated whether the odds are sufficiently in your favour before you commit yourself*
- *After you have placed your bet, do not be afraid to cut a loss if the trend turns against you*
- *The first cut is the cheapest cut, and you must be prepared to take quick and ruthless action.*

FUTURES BASED BETS ON AN INDIVIDUAL SHARE

Start by looking at the charts of the constituent companies that make up the FTSE 100. These shares are traded more often than the others, and so the spreads are likely to be narrower than the shares in the FTSE 250 or 350. When you have found the pattern that looks right, investigate the share in more detail.

■ *The best pattern to find is one where the share price's recent historical movement is following a general trend at an angle of 45 degrees, either upwards or downwards*

■ *Establish the trading range*

■ *Calculate whether there is enough movement within the trading range in money terms to cover the spreads (both opening and closing) as well as to show you a profit*

■ *Check whether there is enough room between the current price and the next resistance or support level to make a profit*

■ *If you are contemplating a buy bet, wait until the share price has turned upwards, before opening the bet*

■ *If you are contemplating a sell bet, wait until the share price has turned downwards, before opening the bet*

■ *Check when the next interim or final figures will be announced, and if they will fall in the period whilst the bet is running, read all the press comment about the analysts' expectations of profit levels (or profit/loss warnings)*

■ *Check whether the expected results are already discounted in the price or not*

■ *Always give yourself enough time for the price to move sufficiently to give you the profit you are seeking. If there is only one month, or less before the 'near future' expires, base your bet on the one after that. Very often there will not be that much difference in the quotations between the two dates*

- *Never look back. Hindsight is 20/20 vision. Don't let it cloud your judgement for the next bet. Stick to your risk/return principles and only bet when all the criteria have been satisfied. The amateur loses money by betting too often. Bet sparingly, and only when you are completely satisfied that the odds are in your favour. Adopt a questioning attitude to the facts, rather than persuading yourself that the facts can be interpreted more favourably than logic suggests. Hope springs eternal, but the bill for reality is presented daily, and it has to be paid.*

HOW TO CALCULATE THE ODDS

We shall use Fig 8.1 to illustrate how to calculate the odds. In this case we shall be contemplating opening a buy bet.

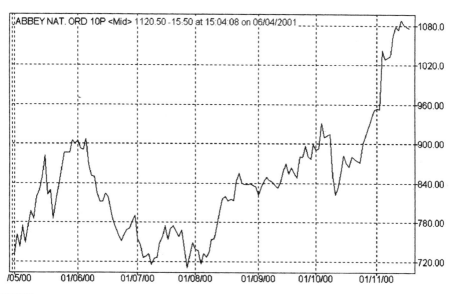

FIG 8.1 Using trends to calculate the odds

Starting at the share price level of 790p, around 12 August 2000, the picture would have been well into the formation of the classic cup shape that started at the beginning of June that year. The trading range had established itself between 720p and 785p, but then there was a price break out upwards. So the question remains what are the odds in favour of the price going to the next resistance level? There is a minor resistance level at around 800p, and the odds in favour of hitting that level are very strongly in your favour. However, the next major resistance level occurs at around 900p. Depending on what the price does at the 800p level, the odds will alter either way.

There is not enough upside potential in the price movement to open a buy bet at 790p to warrant the risk of a downturn at that level, so the odds in your favour are insufficient and you should wait and see what happens to the price movement after it has reached 800p.

When it continued to rise above the 800p level, the odds in your favour of the price going to 900p became very strong indeed, and it would be sensible to open a buy bet straight away, As the price rises towards the 900p level, the odds against it going through the 900p level weaken for every additional increase in the price.

You can see that exactly the same calculation can be applied to a falling price. Don't forget that prices tend to fall twice as fast as they rise, so you need to be very quick indeed to maximize your odds for success in a falling market or share price.

■ RISK WARNING

'Spreadbets carry a high degree of risk to your capital. Only speculate with money you can afford to lose. Prices may move rapidly against your interests and resulting losses may require further payments to be made. Spread betting may not be suitable for all investors. Therefore ensure you fully understand the risks involved and seek independent advice if necessary.' This risk warning is published by 'deal4free', and it sums up the warning and advice concisely.

> Only speculate with money you can afford to lose

In this book we have shown you how to limit risks as far as possible, but when all is said and done, it is you who makes the decisions as to how much of your capital you put at risk. We have shown you how to exercise control of your investments in financial spread betting.

Good luck, and good hunting!

➤ Summary

In this chapter we have examined:

- the checklist you need to follow before you commit yourself to opening a bet on an index;
- the checklist you need to follow before you commit yourself to opening a bet on a futures based individual share;
- how to calculate whether there is enough likely movement in the share price to cover the costs of the spread and make a sufficient profit; and
- how to calculate the odds before you place a bet.

APPENDIX 1

Market information

List of the markets and instruments against which financial spread bets can be placed generally. The amounts of the spread, and the minimum and maximum stakes accepted will vary from one bookmaker to another, so the figures given here are meant as a guide only. You must confirm actual limits and spreads and stake sizes with your bookmaker. They can vary quite a lot.

INTRADAY BETS

	Trading hours	Min-max bet size £	Bet per	Spread	Bet size factor	Contract months
FTSE 100	0700–2130	2–500	1 index point move in futures price	6–8	250	Mar, Jun, Sept, Dec
Wall Street	0700–2130	2–500	1 index point move in futures price	12–14	350	Mar, Jun, Sept, Dec
S&P 500	0700–2130	2–500	0.1 index point move in futures price	1.4	350	Mar, Jun, Sept, Dec

STOCK INDICES – INTRADAY BETS

	Trading hours	Min-max bet size £	Bet per	Spread	Bet size factor	Contract months
FTSE 100	0700–2130	2–500	1 index point move in futures price	10	250	Mar, Jun, Sept, Dec
Wall Street	0700–2130	2–500	1 index point move in futures price	14	350	Mar, Jun, Sept, Dec
S&P 500	0700–2130	2–500	0.1 index point move in futures price	1.4	350	Mar, Jun, Sept, Dec
FTSE/ Wall Street Differential	0700–2130	2–500	1 index point move in futures price	22	350	Mar, Jun, Sept, Dec
CAC 40	0700–2130	2–500	1 index point move in futures price	8	150	every month
DAX 30	0740–1600	2–500	1 index point move in futures price	8	200	Mar, Jun, Sept, Dec
IBEX 35	0900–1615	1–250	1 index point move in futures price	24	200	every month
MIB 30	0830–1630	0.5–100	1 index point move in futures price	100	1500	Mar, Jun, Sept, Dec
OMX	0900–1600	2–250	1 index point move in futures price	8	200	every month
Swiss market	0730–1555	2–250	1 index point move in futures price	10	200	Mar, Jun, Sept, Dec
Nikkei Dow 225	0700–2115	0.5–100	1 index point move in futures price	80	1000	Mar, Jun, Sept, Dec
Hang Seng	0700–1600	1–100	1 index point move in futures price	70	750	every month
NASDAQ	0700–2115	2–100	0.1 index point move in futures price	40	400	Mar, Jun, Sept, Dec
Amsterdam Index	0830–1530	2–100	1 index point move in futures price	6	100	every month when liquid
STOXX 50	0900–1600	2–100	1 index point move in futures price	8	150	Mar, Jun, Sept, Dec
FTSE Eurotop 100	0900–1600	2–100	1 index point move in futures price	16	150	Mar, Jun, Sept, Dec

	Trading hours	Min-max bet size £	Bet per	Spread	Bet size factor	Contract months
RTX	0800–1515	2–100	1 index point move in futures price	16	40	every month when liquid
HTX	0900–1500	2–100	1 index point move in futures price	16	100	every month when liquid
ATX	0800–1400	2–100	1 index point move in futures price	16	100	every month when liquid
BEL 20	0830–1545	2–100	1 index point move in futures price	8	200	every month when liquid
Industrial index	0700–1530	2–100	1 index point move in futures price	40	300	Mar, Jun, Sept, Dec

■ DAILY BETS

	Trading hours	Min-max bet size £	Bet per	Spread	Bet size factor	Contract months
Daily FTSE 100	0700–2130	2–500	1 index point move in daily price	7	100	n/a
Daily Wall Street	0700–2100	2–500	1 index point move in daily price	9	200	n/a
Daily CAC 40 Future	0700–1600	2–500	1 index point move in daily price	6	75	n/a
Daily DAX 30 Future	0740–1600	2–500	1 index point move in daily price	6	100	n/a

CURRENCIES

	Trading hours	Min-max bet size £	Bet per	Spread	Bet size factor	Contract months
EURO/ Sterling (pounds to one euro)	0700–2130	1–500	0.0001 move in futures price (i.e. 0.7100)	20	150	Mar, Jun, Sept, Dec
EURO/USD (US dollars to one euro)	0700–2130	1–500	0.0001 move in futures price (i.e. 1.1950)	30	200	Mar, Jun, Sept, Dec
EURO/J.Yen (J.Yens to) one euro	0700–2130	1–500	0.01 move in futures price (i.e. 130.00)	30	200	Mar, Jun, Sept, Dec
EURO/ Swiss Francs (Swiss francs to one euro)	0700–2130	1–500	0.0001 move in futures price (i.e. 1.6250)	30	200	Mar, Jun, Sept, Dec
USD/ Swiss Francs (Swiss francs to $1)	0700–2130	1–500	0.0001 move in futures price (i.e. 1.4450)	30	200	Mar, Jun, Sept, Dec
USD/J.Yen (J.Yens to $1)	0700–2130	1–500	0.01 move in futures price (i.e. 116.50)	30	200	Mar, Jun, Sept, Dec
I.M.M. British Pound	0700–2130	1–500	0.0001 move in futures price (i.e. 1.6500)	30	200	Mar, Jun, Sept, Dec
I.M.M. Deutsche Mark	0700–2130	1–500	0.0001 move in futures price (i.e. 0.5950)	12	100	Mar, Jun, Sept, Dec
I.M.M. J.Yen	0700–2130	1–500	0.000001 move in futures price (i.e. 0.008504)	18	150	Mar, Jun, Sept, Dec
I.M.M. Swiss Franc	0700–2130	1–500	0.0001 move in futures price (i.e. 0.6920)	12	100	Mar, Jun, Sept, Dec

	Trading hours	Min-max bet size £	Bet per	Spread	Bet size factor	Contract months
I.M.M. French Franc	0700–2130	1–500	0.00001 move in futures price (i.e. 0.17860)	30	200	Mar, Jun, Sept, Dec
I.M.M. Canadian	0700–2130	1–500	0.0001 move in futures price (i.e. 0.7560)	12	100	Mar, Jun, Sept, Dec
I.M.M. Australian $	0700–2130	1–500	0.0001 move in futures price (i.e. 0.6530)	12	100	Mar, Jun, Sept, Dec
Sterling/ J.Yen (J.Yens to £1)	0700–2130	1–500	0.01 move in futures price (i.e. 120.00)	40	200	Mar, Jun, Sept, Dec
Sterling/ Swiss Franc (Swiss francs to £1)	0700–2130	1–500	0.0001 move in futures price (i.e. 2.1500)	40	200	Mar, Jun, Sept, Dec

▮ BONDS

	Trading hours	Min-max bet size £	Bet per	Spread	Bet size factor	Contract months
US 30 yr T-BOND	0700–2130	2–500	1/32nd move in futures price	6/32nds	64	Mar, Jun, Sept, Dec
US 10yr T-Notes	0700–2130	2–500	1/32nd move in futures price	6/32nds	64	Mar, Jun, Sept, Dec
US 5yr T-Notes	0700–2130	2–500	12/64th move in futures price	12/64ths	64	Mar, Jun, Sept, Dec
UK 30yr Gilt	0800–1800	2–500	1 tick move in futures price	6	100	Mar, Jun, Sept, Dec
Japanese 10 yr Govt. Bond	07.00–1600	2–500	1 tick move in futures price	8	100	Mar, Jun, Sept, Dec
German 10yr Bund	0700–1800	2–500	1 tick move in futures price	6	100	Mar, Jun, Sept, Dec

▶

	Trading hours	Min-max bet size £	Bet per	Spread	Bet size factor	Contract months
German 5yr Bobl	0700–1800	2–500	1 tick move in futures price	6	100	Mar, Jun, Sept, Dec
Italian 10yr Bond (BTP)	0700–1758	2–500	1 tick move in futures price	8	100	Mar, Jun, Sept, Dec
French 10yr Notional Bond (PTB)	0700–1800	2–500	1 tick move in futures price	8	100	Mar, Jun, Sept, Dec
Spanish 10yr Notional Bond (MEFF)	0800–1615	2–500	1 tick move in futures price	8	150	Mar, Jun, Sept, Dec

INTEREST RATES

	Trading hours	Min-max bet size £	Bet per	Spread	Bet size factor	Contract months
Short Sterling 3mth LIBOR	0805–1605 1622–1757	5–1000	0.01 move in futures price	5	50	Mar, Jun, Sept, Dec
Eurodollar 3mth	0700–1250 1320–2130	5–1000	0.01 move in futures price	5	50	Mar, Jun, Sept, Dec
Euroswiss 3mth	0810–1605 1624–1755	5–1000	0.01 move in futures price	6	50	Mar, Jun, Sept, Dec
Euro (EURIBOR) 3mths	0730–1800	5–1000	0.01 move in futures price	8	50	Mar, Jun, Sept, Dec

▮ OPTIONS

	Trading hours	Min-max bet size £	Bet per	Spread	Bet size factor	Contract months
FTSE options on cash market	0700–2130	5–250	1 index point move in options price	10 min, 30 max	if buy– premium x stake if sell – 250 x stake	every month when liquid
Wall Street Options	1320–2100	5–50	0.1 index point move in options price	30 +	if buy– premium x stake if sell– 350 x stake	Mar, Jun, Sept, Dec
S&P Options	1430–2115	5–250	0.10 move in options price	10 min, 30 max	if buy– premium x stake if sell– 350 x stake	every month when liquid
Bond Options	0732–1600	5–250	0.01 move in options price	10	if buy– premium x stake if sell– 100 x stake	every month when liquid
Gilt Options	0800–1615	5–200	0.01 move in options price	10	if buy– premium x stake if sell– 100 x stake	every month when liquid
US T-Bonds Options	1320–2000	5–200	1/64th move in options price	12/64ths	if buy– premium x stake if sell– 64 x stake	every month when liquid

▶

	Trading hours	Min-max bet size £	Bet per	Spread	Bet size factor	Contract months
Short Sterling Options	0800–1602	5–250	0.01 move in options price	6	if buy– premium x stake if sell– 50 x stake	Mar, Jun, Sept, Dec
I.M.M. GBP/USD Options	1320–2000	3–100	0.0001 move in options price	20	if buy– premium x stake if sell– 200 x stake	Mar, Jun, Sept, Dec
I.M.M. Yen/USD Options	1320–2000	3–100	0.0000001 move in options price	20	if buy– premium x stake if sell– 100 x stake	Mar, Jun, Sept, Dec
I.M.M. Swiss/USD Options	1302–2000	3–100	0.0001 move in options price	20	if buy– premium x stake if sell– 100 x stake	Mar, Jun, Sept, Dec
Gold Options	1320–1930	2–500	$0.1 move in options price	16 ($1.6)	if buy– premium x stake if sell– 150 x stake	Feb, Apr, Jun, Aug, Oct, Dec
Silver Options	1325–1925	5–250	0.5 cent move in options price	3 cents	if buy– premium x stake if sell– 80 x stake	every month when liquid

PRECIOUS METALS

	Trading hours	Min-max bet size £	Bet per	Spread	Bet size factor	Contract months
Gold	0700–1930	1–500	$0.1 move in futures price	16 ($1.6)	150	Feb, Apr, Jun, Aug, Oct, Dec
Silver	0700–1925	1–500	0.5 cent move in futures price	8 (4 cents)	100	Jan, Mar, May, Jul, Sept, Dec
Palladium	1310–1920	1–50	$0.1 move in futures price	14 ($1.4)	100	Mar, Jun, Sept, Dec
Platinum	1320–1930	1–50	$0.1 move in futures price	24 ($2.4)	100	Jan, Apr, Jul, Oct.
High grade	1310–1900	1–50	$0.01 move in futures price	80	500	Jan, Mar, May, Jul, Sept, Dec

COMMODITIES

	Trading hours	Min-max bet size £	Bet per	Spread	Bet size factor	Contract months
Corn	1530–1915	5–50	0.25 cent move in futures price	3 cents	80	Mar, May, Jul, Sept, Dec
Soyabeans	1530–1915	5–25	0.25 cent move in futures price	4 cents	100	Jan, Mar, May, Jul, Aug, Sept, Nov
Soyabean meal	1530–1915	5–25	0.10 cent move in futures price	14 cents ($1.4)	100	Jan, Mar, May, Jul, Aug, Sept, Oct, Dec
Soyabean oil	1530–1915	2–50	0.01 cent move in futures price	20 (0.2 cents)	100	Jan, Mar, May, Jul, Aug, Sept, Oct, Dec
Wheat	1530–1915	5–25	0.25 cent move in futures price	3 cents	100	Mar, May, Jul, Sept, Dec

▶

	Trading hours	Min-max bet size £	Bet per	Spread	Bet size factor	Contract months
New York Cocoa	1330–1830	3–150	$1 move in futures price	14	60	Mar, May, Jul, Sept, Dec
Robusta Coffee	0945–1230 1415–1700	3–50	$1 move in futures price	14	50	Jan, Mar, May, Jul, Sept, Nov
Coffee	1415–1832	20–300	0.1 cent move in futures price	14 (1.4 cents)	100	Mar, May, Jul, Sept, Dec
Sugar No. 5	0945–1830	3–50	0.1 cent move in futures price	14 ($1.4)	75	Mar, May, Aug, Oct, Dec
Sugar No. 11	1430–1820	5–200	0.01 cent move in futures price	10 (0.1 cents)	50	Mar, May, Jul, Oct
Orange juice	1515–1915	1–25	0.01 cent move in futures price	120 (1.2 cents)	350	Jan, Mar, May, Jul, Sept, Nov

■ OIL PRODUCTS

	Trading hours	Min-max bet size £	Bet per	Spread	Bet size factor	Contract months
Brent Crude Oil	1002–2013	5–500	1 cent move in futures price	6 cents	100	every month
Light Crude Oil	1445–2010	5–250	1 cent move in futures price	6 cents	100	every month
Gas Oil	0915–1727	10–250	0.25 cent move in futures price	4 ($1.00)	40	every month

Useful addresses

Financial bookmakers

Cantor Index Limited
1 America Square
London EC3N 2LS
tel: 020 7894 8800

City Index Limited
Park House
Finsbury Circus
London EC2M 7PQ
tel: 020 7861 5555

CMC Spreadbet Plc
Bayley Hall
Queens Road
Hertford SG14 1EN
tel: 08000 933 633 (UK Freephone)
website: www.deal4free.com/spreadbet
e-mail: info@deal4free.com

Financial Spreads Limited
46 Cannon Street
London EC4N 6JT
tel: 0800 0969620
website: www.finspreads.com

IFX
2 America Square
London EC3N 2LU
tel: 020 7892 0916
or 0845 1000 700
website: www.ifxfinancial.com

I G Index Plc
Friars House
157–168 Blackfriars Road
London SE1 8EZ
tel: 0800 195 3100 (freephone) or 020 7896 0011
website: www.igindex.co.uk

Spreadex Ltd
Freepost ANG 7156
PO Box 4116
Dunstable LU6 1YT
tel: 0800 0526575
website: www.spreadex.co.uk

Advisory service
Internet Sporting Club Limited and Share Raider
Riverside Business Centre
River Lawn Road
Tonbridge
Kent TN9 1EP
tel: 01732 783532
website: www.internetsportsclub.co.uk
or www.shareraider.co.uk

Software
Update Software Plc
Updata House
Old York Road
London SW18 1TG
tel: 020 8874 4747
website: www.updata.co.uk

Index